Being Gay is Not all Fabulous

Short stories of black South African gay men

Katlego Vincent Scheepers (Ed)

Hoopoe Press

Being Gay is Not all Fabulous: Short stories of black South African gay men

Published by UJ Press under the Hoopoe Press imprint
University of Johannesburg
Library
Auckland Park Kingsway Campus
PO Box 524
Auckland Park
2006
https://ujonlinepress.uj.ac.za/

Compilation © Katlego Vincent Scheepers 2023
Chapters © Authors 2023
Published Edition © Katlego Vincent Scheepers 2023

First published 2023

https://doi.org/10.36615/9781776438815

978-1-7764388-0-8 (Paperback)
978-1-7764388-1-5 (PDF)
978-1-7764388-2-2 (EPUB)
978-1-7764388-3-9 (XML)

This publication had been submitted to a rigorous double-blind peer-review process prior to publication and all recommendations by the reviewers were considered and implemented before publication.

Copy editor: Kyleigh Greatorex
Cover design: Hester Roets, UJ Graphic Design Studio
Typeset in 10/13pt Merriweather Light

Contents

Prologue i
Katlego Vincent Scheepers

1   Negotiating spaces: Confronting myriad
experiences 1
Katlego Vincent Scheepers

2   Defying heteronormativity: A black gay man's
experiences in a heteropatriarchal rural space 9
Tshepo Maake

3   The people you associate yourself with can either
break or build you, watch out! 27
Itumeleng Serobe

4   My journey to becoming 33
Xola Dladla-Nkosi

5   The Brotherhood 39
Obakeng Pholo

6   Mommy Knows, So Who Cares? 49
Lerato Mofokeng

7   Breathe 57
Olebogeng Seripe

Letters to our younger selves 65

Definition of concepts 77

Acknowledgements 79

Contributors 81

Prologue

Katlego Vincent Scheepers

We cannot underestimate how critical stories are, especially those told by ourselves. These stories enable us to reflect and carve new possibilities for ourselves, as well as impart knowledge on those who come after us. Given its importance, it is pertinent to ask, how can stories shape how we view life and what can we learn from these experiences? Albert Einstein states, "the only source of knowledge is experience".

Reflecting on my story and reading the stories in this book reminds me what it took for gay men to be recognised in some settings. As I page through these narratives, I am reminded of the many that risked their lives and are unfortunately no longer with us. Harvey Milk famously said that "all young people, regardless of their sexual orientation, or identity, deserve a safe and supportive environment in which to achieve their full potential" and many have been robbed of that privilege.

We, as a society, can agree that homophobia and transphobia are not uncommon. Many Lesbian, Gay, Bisexual, Trans and Queer, Intersex (LGBTQI+) persons resort to taking their lives or are brutally murdered at an inappropriately high rate across the globe and it is no surprise that homophobia and transphobia continue to thrive and go unchecked.

This homophobia and transphobia have been a backdrop of my life. Growing up in Potchefstroom (North West Province, South Africa) was not always easy, but I was fortunate to have my parents who brought me up the way they did.

Borrowing from **JUST** the title *I Write What I Like* by Steve Biko, these short stories provide raw personal accounts of gay men in South Africa. What these stories offer are real life accounts, focusing on their sexual orientation, providing lessons learnt and in some way illustrating real determination and a zest to live. At the core of narrating their personal accounts, what can be appreciated is the language they use. In Higher Education, there have been many talks on decolonisation and by the way these stories are narrated, I believe they add to this project, showing how Africans think and feel.

Many a time, Africans have been told how to think and feel, especially, when using English as a medium of communication; but what purpose does it serve to write in a foreign language that many, particularly those in our communities, may not understand? To address societal problems, notably at a grassroot level, it is important to write in a language that the intended audience may understand.

To avoid our stories being told by someone else without providing context, I believe it is important to allow South Africans, especially those not established to write in the "not so sophisticated" English they prefer and will understand. This, I believe, will encourage contributors to pen their perspectives in the way they understand and will further avoid the erosion of our culture. We should think and write in a language that we will understand. For change to occur, especially for the LGBTIQ+ community, Africans need to be encouraged to express themselves, even in a language that in many spaces might not be deemed "sophisticated". The narratives provide the true expression of the contributors.

As I ponder upon change in our societies, I am reminded of an unpublished poem by Thatto Otlotleng Tshipo titled "The Little Boy".

I've always been afraid to confront the enemy head-on.

Maybe because I have been conditioned to never question any means of authority or power – self-proclaimed, feeding off the marginalised to maintain its systematic dominance or whatever its root.

Mine is a reflection of yours, yours is a reflection of mine – let's not let prejudice be this retraction only you and I can combine, refine and align.

Why does my freedom call for revolutionary marches?
Why is my identity politicised and twisted into your
one-sided agenda?
Why do preconceived notions of who I am cause such resistance to
claim my place in society?
It's us versus ourselves
It's us burying the loud voices that desire emancipation

Freedom from the shackles of social conditioning
It's the right wing verses the left
Conscience verses greed
Creed verses love
Hearts verses heads
Historical divisions that have left festering wounds.

To the little black boy curled up in his arms, questioning why his light
cannot be seen, acknowledged and embraced with open hearts,
I see you. I see your blazing heart
I hear your cries
I hear your burning questions and uncertainties

Why does your femininity have to contradict notions of masculinity in
an unsolicited path society has predetermined for you?
Remember it's us verses ourselves
It's us burying the loud voices that desire emancipation

Freedom from the shackles of social conditioning
Healing cycles of detrimental thinking
It's the right wing verses the left
Conscience verses greed
Creed verses love

I've said my part. I've exercised my freedom of expression.
Now let queer lives live on to express their own.

In my chapter, I confront the myriad experiences of my sexual
identity and the constant struggle of being a young, black gay
man in South Africa. In chapter two, Tshepo sheds insight on
how social norms establish the status of each gender category

by establishing rules and procedures, but regrettably these norms exclude individuals who are viewed as the "other." In his reflection, he states "I did not deserve to grow up in a setting where I was compelled to take on and internalise a heterosexual gender, and the struggle for 'normalcy' and establishing manhood was never my battle to wage." This chapter challenges us all to start accepting and being receptive to the notion that gay men are not an exception.

Chapter three is a reflection of Itumeleng describing how his mother always encouraged him to take responsibility for his actions and to understand that they may have either positive or negative results. Although he had his mother and brother on his side, he believed that academics would give him a voice in their absence. In chapter four, Xola also considers his successes in sports, choir, and dancing as some of the ways he was able to survive the bullying. He observes that, particularly for gay people, growing up in Soweto was not easy.

It is interesting how gay men were constantly encouraged to be friends with other males in their younger years (primary and high school), but they later discovered that they could not relate to this required manly behaviour. In chapter five, Obakeng states that "There weren't many gay boys at my school; in fact, nobody was gay, as I sit back and reflect". Obakeng makes us think of gay men's fraternity that develops after matriculation. He writes that we unexpectedly cross paths.

In chapter six, Lerato shares a moving and heart-breaking story of grief. He reflects on the recent passing of his mother, a pillar of support. In the final chapter, Olebogeng encourages us to breathe. We have all encountered challenges along this journey called life. What Olebogeng urges us to do is to have patience. He encourages us to not let the current situation define us. The only way to find hope is to look to the future.

As we move towards a more inclusive South Africa, one that celebrates all sexual identities, the time has come for our society to reconcile and rebuild itself while advocating love and acceptance. Gay men are often expected to be fabulous, all the while carrying long-lasting scars of being judged and outcasted. This book was inspired by my constant desire to find a book of hope that was easily understandable by everyone and was written by a person I could relate to. *Being Gay is Not ALL Fabulous* is a collection of stories about our past experiences, myths, encounters, love, loss, and aspirations for the future. The constant media coverage; images of colourful and flamboyant gay men depict many gay men as FABULOUS, yet, the dark truth or reality is that many gay men do not have the luxury of living fabulous lives, nor do they have fabulous experiences.

Reading a book can sometimes bring back a lot of memories we thought we had forgotten. There are many different topics, tones, and situations in this book. The stories display an intimate knowledge of gay people and gives a voice to this sexual minority group. The book concludes with letters each contributor has written to their younger selves.

1

Negotiating spaces: Confronting myriad experiences

Katlego Vincent Scheepers

What I would describe as critical moments of my identity are often characterised by moments of ostracism. Of course, this is a personal experience of sexual and racial subjectification. It is made more challenging given the common accusations of being "flamboyant", "sensitive" and sometimes "paranoid". The LGBTIQ+ community in South Africa and elsewhere struggle with myriad experiences of homophobia and transphobia. I would argue that part of the dilemma has to do with practices of exclusion from the society. It has to do with an almost invisible nature of hetero-hegemonic traditions within societies that work to reinforce and sustain patriarchal spaces and traditions that are exclusive to already marginalised bodies. These traditions and practices are so invisible as to render any challenge and resistance almost impossible because one would first have to understand the work of the invisible. In such a context where these practices characterise how the LGBTIQ+ community navigate communities, the question becomes, how do we engage denigrating moments of representation of our bodies in a context that does not allow the representation of queer bodies? I want to argue that some of the important spaces of such navigation and representation occur at different levels, but in my experience, it started when I was still in primary school, or maybe even before that.

The formal and informal social networks that exist in communities function to reinstate hegemonic ways of being where queer bodies are deployed in ways that insult their dignity. I am a black, gay man. My early formative years were nurtured in Potchefstroom, an academic city in the North West Province of South Africa. I have often had to confront the different moments of exclusion. I have experienced my identity as being a person out-of-place. This is not a unique story. I have interacted with many gay and lesbian individuals who have shared similar stories of exclusion back in Potchefstroom and here in Johannesburg, South Africa's biggest city and capital of Gauteng province, where I am currently based. My multiple and intersectional positioning has meant occupying ambiguous statuses at different points in my life. Below I describe some of these critical moments.

Narrative moments

I stored my pain right here inside this suitcase. I struggled to identify myself throughout my childhood. While people perceive me as someone strong and resilient, they are unaware that I occasionally have to drown in my own sorrows considering the life I had. My anxiety is a contributing factor to some of my pain. The fact that I am constantly misunderstood and misrepresented greatly contributes to this anxiety. I have had many instances where people would misrepresent what I stand for. Thus, after 12 years of schooling I vowed to never have to explain myself. It is so sad that many gay men find themselves in this position where they have to constantly explain themselves.

Primary and high school

Because I was continually reminded that I am not "normal", primary school was a misery for me. I used to get the label "gay" from people, but I had no idea what that really meant. At the time, I thought that being gay meant dressing up, applying makeup, and having hair styled like a girl and someone who aspires to female status. Growing up, I was always reminded that "boys are assertive, play with cars, want to be with women". I have always associated the colour pink with girls and blue with boys.

I remember, my daily prayer was to blend in and behave "normal" so that no one would notice me. So, when I was elected prefect in Grade 7, that devastated me! The fact that I would occasionally have to reprimand *boys* caused a lot of anxiety. The fear that I would be reminded of my sexual orientation was the source of my uneasiness. An expression used with such disdain. One thing I want people to understand is that being gay has a stigma that is unfavourable, silences you, and prevents people from engaging with your true self. Because belonging is important to us, it makes one feel as though they do not belong. We look to the outside world for approval (parents, teachers, school children etc). We need someone to reassure us that we are "normal," valid, and are a part of something. Today, I can genuinely affirm that I lacked this. I had to constantly assume this patriarchal male persona, which at the time, was difficult because it meant I had to follow the rulebook. As I'm reflecting and thinking back on that time, I'm filled with rage and despair.

For me, high school was just like primary school – emotionally draining! I attended an all-boys high school. I now understand that such places enforce patriarchy and hegemonic masculinity! You are constantly watched, down to the way you walk and speak! In Grade 8, I made an effort to isolate myself, but I didn't want to do it too much because doing so would have made me more vulnerable to bullying; which did happen. I continued to be friends with those I went to primary school with. But as time went on, I began interacting with two more folks. For me, Tim and Nathan served as my safe haven from the toxic environment. Our friendship became very strong after we had each confessed our sexuality (being gay) to each other thinking the other didn't know. What we all had in common was that we dated girls. We undoubtedly visualised a future with these women. Growing up in that time, I realised myself and others were forced to want this reality of having a partner and being promiscuous because you are surrounded by boys and attend a school that strongly supports hegemonic masculinity. We were taught in school to treat women as though they are weak and in need of male protection. They must have followed the bible because the school was founded on Christian principles. I don't mean to imply that the bible is flawed, but I do want to urge leaders to avoid inflicting harm, especially on children, through its use. Yes, perhaps patriarchy was effective in the past. Now, it is not functional. Some of the customary traditions must also adapt in light of how the world is developing. Old solutions won't work to fix a new issue. And I discovered this as I left the school in November 2012 after completing my third English exam. I made a commitment to myself that I would be true to myself and fight for what I believe in.

University

Going into university, I had an idea of how the next three years were going to play out. This meant that I was going to make up for the time I had lost. I was going to nurture myself and do exactly what I wanted. But I soon realised that life does not always go as you plan.

I had to get a university degree and get a job. I figured that my parents would throw me out once they started realising that I was not in a "phase". I feared being thrown out because of the "shame" of having a gay son would bring to my entire family. "My parents are going to be mad and throw me out!" This was always on my mind. But I also could not fail myself yet again. I could not take the pain.

All I ever wanted was to present my authentic self in a way I wanted to. The good thing about the university space is that you see a lot of LGBTIQ+ individuals and that encourages you to be yourself. It is liberating! And so, third year came – and I knew that I wanted to move. I wanted to leave Potchefstroom and start life somewhere. Johannesburg was obviously my first choice because it was close to home. So, I had to make sure that I do well in my third year so that I could move and that's exactly what I did. In January 2016, I took a taxi to Johannesburg, and this was a defining moment for me.

Moving to Johannesburg

I relocated to Johannesburg in that suitcase you saw. I discovered myself and realigned my goals. I became aware of the value of money. With so many things, I had to improvise. Understanding that mom is serious when she says she doesn't have money required a new kind of understanding for me. One day, as I was returning from university, anxious and fatigued, I noticed my landlord's car parked outside the commune. I was abruptly reminded that I owed rent. I returned to campus and remained there until after seven o'clock, when I was certain he had left. I don't even remember what time I went to sleep since all I can recall was going to my room and crying so hard. That I had to experience this on my own in a foreign place seemed so unjust. I was aware that calling my mother would stress her. So, I simply went to bed and promised myself that I would rise early and return late to avoid my landlord. This went on for about a week before I summoned the guts to phone my mother, who right away came up with a plan and sent the money for rent.

I've developed my capacity for resiliency, perseverance, and fierce self-defence. When I decided to end my life in March 2017, I sought to see a psychologist, and I remember her telling me that "I have come too far to let it all go away". She further asked why I think suicide is the ultimate goal and whether it would make me happy. Of cause, this was not what I wanted to hear, but after that conversation, I remember sitting myself down and really questioning the essence of my existence and I am glad I did not go through with it.

From that moment, I vowed to myself that I would pursue a PhD. Being the first person in my immediate family to ever go to university, I knew I had to seize the opportunity. Our little family was always looked down upon when I was a child. My parents were left out of the decision-making process. One thing I've discovered is that despite all this, my parents managed to keep the family together. My mother taught us to love and enjoy the journey; bask in the little precious moments in life that do not require money. This principle has taught me to appreciate everything in my life.

So, shortly after the visit to my therapist, I recall spending two months in Johannesburg without a place to stay. I used to sleep on campus (UJ). But I soon realised that I was not the only one. There are many of us who slept in toilets, malls and on campus. We suffered in silence.

Because I was a tutor, this meant that even when I was in front of my students I could not burst into tears. I occasionally felt tears forming in my eyes and hastily wiped them away. It is challenging when other people look up to you for support and you feel too weak to even support yourself. One thing that helped me persevere was the awareness that I could not let my students down and wanted them all to get distinctions in Sociology – for some, it was their first time. This meant that I would have to pack these emotions into the black suitcase.

Beyond my mother and sister's support and love, education has always been key to my success. For me, I believe obtaining a PhD will open doors that will allow me to alter the circumstances at home. I believe knowledge is power. I listen to Les Brown, an American politician and motivational speaker and read books by the likes of Robin Sharma, a Canadian writer. From these I have learned that hard work pays off.

This process has also shown me that if you want to make a difference in the world, one ought to empower themselves with education. I want to encourage the young and old out there to never give up. When you start something, make it a point that you finish it. This builds character! A character that will follow through as you journey through life. Finally, as societies, let us make a difference by understanding and being able to interpret situations so that we may be able to grasp the essence of the dialogues.

Conclusion

In sharing my story, I wish to highlight the important fact that black gay men who have an unquenchable thirst to live a life free of homophobia still walk among us. Many a times, these men commit suicide or die at the hands of perpetrators who still maintain traditional ethos of patriarchy. I have, from day one, felt that I do not belong in a world that does not celebrate and embrace queer lives. This is why I am sharing my personal story to, at the very least, encourage whoever reading this piece right now to reflect on the ongoing hate crime and to make a small positive change to ending it. For us to feel that the world is for us, and for us to achieve the yearned sense of belonging, it is crucial that we share stories without fear or favour.

2

Defying heteronormativity: A black gay man's experiences in a heteropatriarchal rural space

Tshepo Maake

Social norms dictate how gender should be performed through rules and guidelines that determine the status of each gender category. The privileges and responsibilities that a man or woman status possess are subject to social norms, which are transferred through interactions from one generation to the next. When a male is ascribed a role of a man, there are guidelines, rules and norms that he is expected to follow. It is only if he conforms to the normative gender expectations that he is given the status of being a man. Contentions arise when he does not conform to the rules, guidelines, and behaviours predetermined for a man's assigned role. That status is then taken away from him because he fails to meet the societal expectations that sustain the role of being a man. He is labelled a gender "delinquent" and punished through exclusion. Heteronormative understandings of gender in society dictate that men and women should see each other as opposites, and their behaviours and feelings should align with the normative rules that define their ascribed gender.

Growing up as a gay boy in a rural community, where gender and sexuality were only understood in heteronormative terms, I experienced conflicts between who I was and what the community expected me to be. I sought to achieve the status of being a "real" black man who, according to the normative expectations, was heterosexual, masculine, respectable and dominant. This man would marry a woman, bear children, and provide for his family.

When I was 14 years old, I decided to go to initiation school where I would learn about manhood and come back as a "real" man. It was on a winter Sunday, and we had just returned from church with my grandmother and my mother when the decision was finalised. I heard the night before that my brother went to initiation school to become a man. On our way to church, I told my grandmother that I also wanted to go. She discussed it with my mother, uncle, and grandfather, who agreed and gave the needed permission. My mother chose a blanket that I would take with me, and they asked me to choose an old t-shirt and pants that I no longer needed. My uncle called his cousin, who would accompany us to the initiation school. It was a long walk across the village and eventually entering a forest. We walked through the thorny trees of the forest until we reached a destination closer to the initiation school. Two men approached us, and I was told to stay behind as my uncle and his cousin went to speak to these men. After a little while, I saw one of them walking away while the other one joined and waited with us. I did not know what we were waiting for, but I could hear voices ahead, and I was curious about what would happen next. However, I did not ask any questions; I just sat there under the shade of a tree and listened to their casual chats. I was nervous but also happy that I was finally going to start the process of becoming a man. It started getting dark, and suddenly two men came running; my uncles walked away from me and told me not to be afraid. The two men closed my eyes, held my hand and ran with me. When I opened my eyes, I was surrounded by men, naked, in pain, and I was told that I was a man. That was how I entered the school. I sat on the side, without clothes on and bleeding, and I saw a long queue of boys wearing scattered clothes singing. There was a roaring fire in front of me, and I then knew that the journey to manhood had started.

My decision to go to the initiation school was guided by my desire to prove that I am a "real" man. I spent most of my childhood in a rural community, where I stayed with my grandparents. I was the only child in the house for a while since my sister was born eight years after me and my brother was not living with us. I was interested in playing with dolls, feeding them, bathing them and combing their hair. However, I did not own a lot of dolls since my grandparents only bought me wire cars, marbles, and tennis balls as toys. I only bought dolls once a year when I went on school trips. My grandparents could not afford to pay for all the school trips, so they usually paid for one a year. My grandmother would prepare me a big lunch box in an ice cream container, buy me yoghurt and some chocolates, and then give me R20 to spend on the trip. I would then take that R20 and buy a tiny doll which I would come back with.

While other boys spent time together making their wire cars, my grandfather bought me one from an old man who used to make them. I was not interested in making one for myself. I would usually go to my neighbours and play with their girl child because she owned a lot of dolls and allowed me to play with them as well. When I was not playing with dolls, I would play by myself, wear my grandmother's clothes and her formal church shoes when she was not around. I portrayed what Kopano Ratele (South African psychologist and men and masculinities studies scholar) describes as "non-traditional desires", which refers to "non-conforming desires, practices, identities, relationships, as well as bodies such as what are often called girl-boys, pretty boys, tomboys and intersexed babies, but also instances when a male child wants a pink (anything), or a female child wants to play stick-fighting with boys". According to cultural traditions, my physical male body did not resonate with my *girlish* desires. I was called *mosimanengwanyana* (boy-girl) because my behaviour was described as effeminate and inappropriate for a boy. I could not fit neatly into the boy or girl category because, according to the gender expectations, my body was that of a boy, but my desires and behaviours were those of a girl.

I was reprimanded for playing with girls instead of boys and liking "girl things" and not "boy things". While I was in primary school, I was given girl names, and some boys would make fun of me in front of my classmates. They would sometimes bully me and threaten to hit me when I talked back at them. My second name is Bethuel, and they changed it to Betty to align it with my *girlish* behaviours. The intentions were always wrong. The name-calling went beyond the school environment to the older people in the community. The common Sotho derogatory term used often to describe boys like me was *sempatleng basimaneng*, directly translating to, "do not look for me amongst the boys", which meant that you would only find me amongst the girls. The term emphasised the gender divide between boys and girls, and because I was not portraying the expected qualities of a boy, yet my sex was that of a male, I had to be punished.

In the community, gender, like in many spaces of society, was understood in heteronormative terms, where boys and girls were viewed as opposites and could only be attracted to their opposites, with no other possibilities. Prof Thabo Msibi (a black South African scholar working on issues related to gender and sexuality) alludes to the social constructions of love as a heterosexual experience in rural spaces of the South African society, and this is what we were taught in my rural community. Cultural traditions that separated the initiation of boys and girls into manhood and womanhood taught us to embrace the differences and adhere to the normative prescriptions that dictated who we could fall in love with. The gender differences were highly emphasised in how we were socialised. In Sunday school, we were taught the many stories that alluded to heterosexual marriage as an institution where men could assert their power and women submit to men. Boys and girls were primarily separated in Sunday school, and we were taught that only boys could cross their legs and only girls could sit on the floor with their legs straight. For a boy, sitting with your legs straight indicated that you were lazy; you were supposed to be ready to stand up when they called your name quickly. At school, girls cleaned the floors while boys cleaned the windows. During our traditional ceremonies, young boys assisted older men with slaughtering animals, while young girls helped the older women with cooking. Those traditional cultural ceremonies were guided by strict rules that indicated which part of a slaughtered animal men could eat and which part women could not. When it was time to eat at these traditional ceremonies, the rules directed that young girls sit with the women on the floor, and boys sit on the chairs or benches. The community was strictly embedded into these traditional norms that dictated how males and females should perform the gender roles ascribed to them. Since the community was small, it was relatively easy for people to identify "gender deviants" whose behaviours contradicted the gender order. You could not question cultural traditions or behave in ways that contradict them, because that was seen as disrespect. Thus, my effeminate behaviours and desires were seen to disrespect and undermine the hegemonic status of men in the community, which both men and women highly protected. Being constantly reprimanded was not only an attempt to correct my non-conforming behaviours, but it was also guided by the community's desire to protect the precious dignity of men that would be tainted by the existence of boys with feminine qualities.

"Fixing my gender": Attempting to be "normal"

As young as I was, I understood that I had to change my behaviours to fit in with the other boys. I succumbed to the pressures of the community and sought to align my behaviour to the heteronormative gender expectations. However, I was not only conforming to please the community, but I also genuinely believed that there was something wrong with my behaviour, and I had to fix how I performed my gender. I started playing soccer with boys, a sport that I was never good at and never enjoyed, but I needed to be seen on the soccer field with other boys. I started learning to make wire cars and made friends with boys. Most of the time, the boys would speak about girls and girlfriends, but I was interested in talking about them instead. When we played house by ourselves as boys, I would always choose to be the wife or mother because I was comfortable with the setup of being the wife and having a husband. I was still contradicting the normative gender expectation in a boys' space. At this point, I did not know anything about being gay or what being gay meant, but according to how people in my community used the term, I understood it to mean boys who want to be girls. I was called gay in several instances, and I understood the term to be derogatory. I, therefore, refused to be called gay because I did not feel that I wanted to be a girl, and I wanted the insults to stop. My experience at initiation school made me realise that changing how I behaved and convincing people that I am a "real" man would be a struggle. In the end, I felt that going through initiation was in vain because it did not achieve the purpose. I was detached from the teachings of the initiation school, which were guided by principles of patriarchy that emphasised hegemonic heterosexual masculinity and undermined non-heterosexual masculinities.

Circumcision in the initiation context was not only perceived as an ordinary procedure of removing the foreskin from the penis but also as a process of losing your vulnerability as a young black boy and claiming your position of dominance as a strong black man. Kopano Ratele explains that "in African societies, the significance of a penis to any man's life goes beyond the organ as a physical object". Emphasis is usually placed on the powerful meanings the organ accumulates in different cultures. Thus, the meanings that men attach to their penises and those of other men are decisive elements in how they construct their masculinities. My initiation experience reflects Ratele's argument since most of the teachings were centred around the power of a circumcised penis. Circumcised penises were described as weapons that we would use to dominate women in the bedrooms and outside. We were told that with our penises, we were going to break up families of men who did not undergo initiation because women desired circumcised instead of uncircumcised penises.

In this light, men who did not undergo initiation in the bushes, including those who went through medical circumcision, were perceived as unable to satisfy women sexually. We were taught to see our masculinity as legitimate, compared to other men whose masculinities were vulnerable to questioning because they failed to achieve manhood by undergoing initiation in the bushes. These men were called *mashoboro,* a derogatory Pedi term that meant 'young boy'. *Mashoboro* were perceived as weak and unrespectable men. The term was used in initiation songs to emphasise the power differentials between circumcised and uncircumcised men. As much as I made efforts to fit in, I did not relate to most of the teachings, and much of the time, I felt out of place because the conversations were concentrated on heterosexual relationships, building heterosexual families, having multiple girlfriends, bearing children, resisting female domination, and maintaining a strong voice in the household. I found most of the initiates rude since they called me names, except for one boy who was always kind to me. I was known as the "gay" initiate and felt the unpleasant connotations of shame that accompanied the term. Although I went through the process of initiation, in the eyes of other people in our community, I was still not man enough. Rather than eliminating questions about my gender and getting rid of the "gay" attribute that I did not want to be associated with, initiation intensified the contradictions between my gender and sexual identity. The feelings of discontent intensified when I started high school, where bullying became frequent.

Bullying in high school was characterised by intimidation, and sometimes it got physical, especially from other boys who always provoked me to elicit some reaction that would validate the physical attack on me. I withdrew from interactions with classmates and spent a lot of my time alone, especially in the early years of high school. Through initiation and other interactions with older men, boys in my community were taught to be dominant and assertive. If you did not fight, you were seen as weak. I became a target because my conduct was defined as "feminine". Bullying was used to emphasise my weakness and enforce their dominant masculinities. Although I did not identify myself as a gay boy at that time, the mere perception that I was gay made me vulnerable. Even the manhood that I was supposed to have gained at the initiation school could not protect me from being vulnerable.

I questioned my sexuality because I desired to be a "normal" boy like the other boys.

Falling in love with boys

As I grew older, I started noticing and making friends with people who behaved like me. I met a boy named Lethabo when I was in Grade 10. Lethabo was four years older than me, and he was from the same community, but he moved to Johannesburg with his family. We heard at that time that Johannesburg was gay friendly, and people there were allowed the freedom to be themselves without excessive stigma and discrimination. I met him through Nomsa, a girl from my high school whom he was dating. As much as he was comfortably gay, as he said, he still maintained a heterosexual life when he would come to his family home in the rural areas. He was open about his sex life, and he seemed to have a lot of sexual experiences. He told me stories about multiple men with whom he had engaged in sexual intercourse while in Johannesburg. Lethabo and Nomsa, as are the rest of the names in this story, are fictious names but represents people I know personally.

Interestingly, there were also some men from our rural community he had intercourse with, which was surprising to me because I thought there were only a handful of gay men in the community. I used to spend a lot of time with him. While he was in the rural areas, he stayed with his female cousin, who knew that he was gay and did not have a problem with that. Whenever I visited, we would usually stay indoors, cuddle and kiss. I had minimal sexual experience, and most of the things I knew about sex were those I saw in pornographic pictures. I did not know yet about porn websites; I only knew that I could google black gay porn pictures. Apart from that, some sexual experiences that I had were from playing around with other boys when I was younger. I think I was 11 when we used to play house as young boys, some were wives and some were the husbands. We would touch each other's penises and rub them on each other's butts. I don't even know if this entails a sexual experience since it was just little boys having fun.

The first time I kissed Lethabo was at his home, and I can never forget how uncomfortable I felt. We were sitting on a couch watching music videos, and then he moved closer to me and started stroking my neck. I didn't know whether I was supposed to feel anything from that, but there was nothing, no sensation or any feeling. He moved closer and closer to me until he was in my face. He then started kissing me. My lips started moving. I did not know whether I was doing it right or not, but I knew my lips had to move. We kissed for a few minutes and eventually stopped when I asked for a glass of water. I think I did that because I was very nervous and shaking. After I drank my glass of water, he could not wait to continue. He held my waist and pulled me closer to him. We started kissing again. While we were kissing, he stopped and said, "open your mouth". Now, it dawned on me that I was not doing something right. I started to open my mouth and feel his tongue and saliva in my mouth. I did not know what I was supposed to do with my tongue, so I felt how he moved his tongue inside my mouth, and I started doing the same. The kiss lasted for a while, but it felt a bit uncomfortable because it was my first time, and I did not think I was doing it right. After that day, we started doing it often, and I started getting used to it.

One night Lethabo invited me over to come and sleep at his place. I think I was 16 and had never slept outside my home, but I was "in love", and I wanted to please him. However, I don't think it was love but a mere infatuation. I left home that day without telling anyone that I would not come back. A terrible decision because I got into trouble with my grandparents the following day. When I got to his home, I found him with his cousin drinking whiskey, as always. They both used to drink a lot. They spent most of the money he received from his parents on alcohol. It was around 8 pm when I got there. While we were sitting and watching TV, the cousin's boyfriend came to the house and sat with us for a little while. After a few minutes, they left us on the couch and went to their bedroom. We just sat there, talked and laughed until I suddenly heard loud bangs coming from the cousin's bedroom.

It sounded like something hard hitting the wall repeatedly. He then looked at me and laughed. I asked what was happening; he said, "he is fucking her". I started hearing screams; it was as if they were in the same room with us. They were very loud. I was getting drunk from the whiskey and comfortable, I was not bothered by what was happening in that bedroom. At around 10 pm, we decided to go and sleep. When we got to the other bedroom, we started kissing. He moved from my lips to my neck, and it started feeling good. He was touching my whole body and stroking my butt time and again. He started sucking my nipples, and I felt some pleasure from that. We had already taken off our clothes when we got to bed, but we were still in our underwear. As we were busy touching and kissing, he reached for my underwear and started pulling it down. He then took off his underwear and got on top of me, rubbing his penis against mine. A few minutes into it, he got off me and switched off the light. He reached for lubricant gel and used his fingers to apply it on me. Then he reached for a condom in a drawer on the side of the bed. He put the condom on. We were both silent at the time, and I was not thinking about anything. I was just waiting for the deed to happen. He gently pushed my legs towards my chest and tried pushing his penis inside me. He pushed his penis bit by bit inside of me, and at some point, it started feeling painful and uncomfortable. I pulled back and wanted to stop because the pain was terrible. He asked if he could try again, and I allowed him. He kept on telling me to relax, but the pain was too intense. I could not bear it, so I told him to stop. We stopped, and we slept. It took him just over five minutes to fall asleep, and I hardly slept most of the night. Of course, I was thinking a lot about what had happened, and it was clear to me that I was neither prepared nor ready for intercourse. We did not speak about it before that night, and I did not have anyone to seek some guidance from. The only sex education we got from school involved a girl and a boy, and it was elementary, with very little detail provided. Besides, we were only taught of sex as an awful thing that resulted in unwanted pregnancies and Sexually Transmitted Infections (STIs), not something that one could derive pleasure from. When it came to gay sex, all I knew was from what I observed in porn pictures, which was not sufficient to prepare me for that night. I hardly slept the whole night; I got even to hear our neighbours when they went on their second round and their morning glory. When the morning came, I was ready to leave, but he was enjoying his sleep and did not want to be woken up. I got off the bed, put on my clothes and left him sleeping. I walked alone from his home to mine. I waited for his call the whole day, and he never called. I felt so stupid, and I remember blaming myself for his silence. I did not even know whether to call what happened sex or not because no penetration occurred. That was the first, and the last time I had a bedroom encounter with him. After that, he started being distant, postponing our meetings and eventually, I decided to stop contacting him because I was the only one making efforts for us to meet.

Eventually, my relationship with Lethabo ended, and soon, I started dating his friend, Kamogelo. It was a similar situation to how I met him. I knew the friend through him, but it was intentional because he was planning to hook us up this time. A few weeks after the relationship had ended, I received a call from him, inviting me over for drinks at his house. He told me that he had a couple of friends over and would like me to join them. I went to his house, and when I got there, I found everyone sitting in a circle outside the house, close to the main gate, drinking beers and whisky. I greeted everyone there, grabbed a chair and joined the circle. I noticed a guy sitting next to him, wearing a blue hood, baggy jeans, and a cap. They were holding hands and touching each other. Lethabo introduced me to the boy, "Tshepo, this is Dumisane, my boyfriend from Soshanguve". I was a bit offended that he would do that, considering that in my mind, he and I were once a couple, but I tried not to look bothered and greeted the friend with a smile. When I greeted Kamogelo, Lethabo said, "oh, Kamogelo is single, by the way", while stroking his boyfriend's neck, as he did with mine a couple of weeks before. Kamogelo then asked me to sit next to him. He was from around the area, and he was a few years older than me, a university law student, and he was a bit dark and a lot more masculine. We had great chats and enjoyed the drinks. The night turned out to be a lot of fun. We drank a lot, got drunk, and I kissed Kamogelo. The following day, we were basically a couple, and the four of us would sometimes meet up and spend time together. Kamogelo and I never discussed a lot of sexual dynamics; however, since I was the feminine one, I assumed that I was the "woman" (as society stipulated) in the relationship. He bought me gifts, airtime, and all those nice things, which further asserted my assumption. He was very religious and committed to the church and the lord – a very nice guy, humble and kind. We would usually meet on the streets at night. There was a secluded tree close to a dam that we used to stand under whenever we met. I felt some genuine love with him, and I felt wanted because he showed real interest in me and made time for me. His home was a bit of a walk from my home, but he made efforts to meet me close to my home. Whenever we met, we would kiss and hold each other and tell each other about our undying love for one another. What I found odd was that whenever we kissed in the night, he would reach out to my penis instead of my butt, which raised questions for me because I believed that there was no way he could have been the kind of guy who would have a penis inserted in him.

One night, while Kamogelo was walking me home, we stopped to kiss each other and say our goodbyes, and as we were kissing, I unzipped his pants and touched his penis. It was my very first time going this far, I had only seen it in those gay porn pictures that I had on my phone. It seemed he enjoyed it because he was moaning. After I finished playing with his penis, I stood up to kiss him. He then unzipped my pants and went down on me. There was a lot of sensation, and my penis felt nicely cold as it got wetter from his saliva. He continued for a little while, and I could gather that he was very comfortable doing it, unlike me. That raised many questions for me because I never expected him to do that to me since he was masculine. The relationship went on for about two years. It was over a year into the relationship; I was in matric when I found out that he was previously dating another guy in the community. We had not tried or engaged in penetrative sex with each other, so the sexual roles were still quite blurred. I asked some of the girls I went to school with about his ex-boyfriend and found out that he was involved in multiple sexual relationships with a few other boys. I gathered that he was the giver, meaning he penetrated most of these boys, and obviously, he had penetrated this one that I was dating. He was an ex-convict and I did not find him attractive, but he seemed very lucky with the boys. I did not make a big deal out of the whole issue, and I ignored that my boyfriend was a receiver when he was dating the guy. At some point, I found out that Kamogelo repeatedly cheated on me with his ex. That's when I started asking questions, and to my surprise, he did not even deny that he took it in his butt. I was offended, and I felt stupid because all along, I thought the day we did it, he would be the one penetrating me, but he told me he enjoys receiving. It was strange because I could not understand how a guy like him would want to be penetrated. My understanding was that the feminine ones get penetrated, and the masculine ones penetrate. This is an assumption held by some people in the community, and many gay men have come to believe that this is how it is supposed to be.

From my relationships with these boys, I met other gay boys and started making gay friends. Dumisani and I ironically became friends. He was Kamogelo's neighbour, and through our continued hangouts with the boyfriends, we became close friends. However, he studied in Soshanguve and stayed there with his father. We only saw each other when he visited his mother and grandmother. He was well acquainted with many gay boys, and whenever I would visit him at his father's house, we would hang out with friends. Our contexts were very different because in my rural community, very few people were open about their gay sexual identities, and we could not live openly gay lives because of the stigma attached to homosexuality. Soshanguve was an urban area, a typical South African *township*, and despite some negativity surrounding gay people, there were several people who lived openly as gay. When we used to hang out in the rural area, we knew we could not display public affection, and we could not openly speak about what we did in our bedrooms. Most of our relationships and sexual lives remained hidden. However, we tried to make the best out of the dire situation. We would make friends with other gay guys in the community, hang out together and sometimes go out to local taverns. It was not easy because there were always people who noticed and judged us but fortunately, the discrimination did not get physical. It was mainly in vocal slurs and attacks on personal characters.

When I was in matric, I started becoming comfortable with my sexuality and decided to filter the harmful words people would say about gay people. I decided not to pay attention to the insults anymore, especially when a classmate called me *stabane*, and I became less and less ashamed of being gay. I disclosed this to my mother, and she was not pleased with the news as she objected and told me that it was not possible. The rejection did not stop me from appreciating myself, and I continued to live my gay life behind closed doors. I told her that I would stop dating boys, but I knew I was not going to. I just wanted to please her. When I disclosed this to her, I remember asking if she could not tell that I was gay while growing up based on my feminine behaviours. Her biggest concern was not that I was gay but what people would say when they hear that her son sleeps with boys. It took her just over a year to digest everything and change her thoughts. I had an openly gay friend, Ofentse, who stayed close to my grandmother's house, and he used to visit a lot at home. He was more feminine than me, and my mother assumed we were dating. She was very ill, and my grandmother was taking care of her. I was sitting next to her in the bedroom when she asked, "My son, are you and Ofentse dating". I was caught off-guard, and I did not know how to respond. I wanted to tell her that I was not dating Ofentse, but I am still gay, but scared of her reaction. I then gathered courage and told her the truth. I responded, "no, I am not dating Ofentse, but I am still into guys, and I have a boyfriend". She did not seem shocked, and I remember the exact words she mentioned in her response.

You are my son, and I love you. I have spoken to certain people about your sexual identity, seeking advice, and I have also learned from TV that gay people exist, and it is normal. You have always respected me, and you have never disappointed me. You have always been a well-behaved child, and I am proud of you. I want you to know that I accept you as you, and I want you to live your life in a way that makes you happy, and I hope to see your boyfriend one day (she laughed).

These words changed my life completely, and I still carry them in my heart even today. Her observation from TV was based on a daily *soapie* that we used to watch back in 2009 on SABC 1, called *Generations*. There were two characters, Jason and Senzo, who everyone knew as heterosexual. They worked closely with each other and eventually became lovers, but there was no sign that they were gay, and that is how it got even more interesting. The two guys struggled with being accepted, particularly by Senzo's father, who was rooted in African cultural traditions that condemned gay relationships. The viewers reacted differently to this relationship since others threatened to stop watching the show if it persisted, while others saw it as a validation of gay sexual relations. I was pleased that it had sparked a positive reaction in my mother despite the negativity, to a point where she felt she needed to make peace with who I am and accept me.

While at school, I had heterosexual friends, mostly female, and they were very curious about my gay friends. Some of them started asking questions, and eventually, I gave in and told them the truth about my sexuality. What was interesting to me was the first question they asked me, "Who is the woman and the man between the two of you?" and because my first boyfriend had a girlfriend as well, they argued that I was the woman. I never knew how to explain this because we only kissed, played with each other's penises, and went down on each other. I had not experienced penetration yet and what I understood back then was that in a relationship, there is supposed to be a man and a woman, and perhaps the woman was the one getting penetrated. I found the question compelling because I was exposed to a lot of heterosexual relationships, and I also asked myself the same questions and adhered to that homonormative construction of gay relationships. For some time, I viewed Senzo in the gay relationship from the *soapie* as the woman since he was short and soft-spoken while Jason was tall and assertive. The assumption proved to be wrong, as I learned more about my sexuality outside the confines of the rural space.

Un-doing early socialisations of my gender and sexuality

Through watching the *soapie*, I was exposed to a whole different culture that I never knew could exist. I was experiencing multiple oppressions based on my lack of conformity to normative gender expectations and deviance from a socially prescribed sexuality, and I was being introduced into a culture where gay sexuality is not accompanied by negative connotations. Although there were limitations in how we expressed ourselves publicly due to the heteronormative nature of our community, it felt good to be in a space where I could be myself and not be in constant battles with myself. In my final year of high school, I gave up the battle and accepted that I was never going to fit into the heteronormative gender expectations of a boy and started a new battle of accepting myself as a gay boy because that is who I was. It was a scary and difficult journey because I was not only disrupting the normative gender order by accepting myself as a gay man, but I was also challenging the heteronormativity that, for most of my childhood and teenage years, I sought to conform to. I started questioning my community's heteronormative socialisation of boys and girls into two fixed and opposing gender categories. Fortunately, I was able to escape the rural community and moved to the city to start my tertiary education after completing my matric.

The university space offered me the freedom to explore and construct my identity without worrying about the rural heteronormative gaze that policed and directed my gender throughout my childhood. Most significantly, the university classroom was where I learnt to question heterosexual gender norms and be critical of the social definition of "normal" as an exclusionary term when coming to gender roles. I had to undo the heteronormative constructions of a male gender that I had spent most of my childhood seeking to perfect and reconstruct my gender as a black gay man. My understanding changed, and I took on a different perspective, where I did not have to fit neatly into normative gender specifications that defined the criteria of a real man. The problem with enforcing heteronormative gender identities and limiting the construction of gender to heterosexual categories for all boys is that it ignores the fluidity of gender. Fixing gender to heterosexuality only furthers the oppression of gay men.

The works of Profs Marc Epprecht (a scholar whose research interests are in Africa, gender, sexuality, environmental and social history, colonialism) and Thabo Msibi on gay sexual identities in black communities demonstrate that, African cultural traditions and religion are the two social forces that guide the socialisation of boys and girls in many black communities, and they have been used to justify invalidating non-heterosexual men, including transgender men and other men who do not identify themselves as heterosexual or gay. Similar findings were evident in my research with black gay men, whose experiences of growing up in rural areas indicated cultural traditions and religion as the mechanisms that their community members used to deter the acceptance of sexual minorities. It is imperative to be critical of these two belief systems and how they are used to socialise young boys and girls. In some spaces, they have been used in ways that do more harm than good for gay boys who are constantly confronted with cultures of violence, discrimination and ostracisation. When I disclosed my sexual identity to my parents, I was aware of the possibility that I might be rejected and end up alone. I would not say that it was fortunate for me that after some conflicts between them and myself, and their interactions with other people, they decided to fully accept me as a gay man because that would suggest that being accepted is a privilege. I did not deserve to grow up in a space where I was forced to take on and internalise a heterosexual gender, and the struggle for "normalcy" and proving manhood was never my battle to fight.

3

The people you associate yourself with can either break or build you, watch out!

Itumeleng Serobe

My journey starts as young boy in a small town called Petrus Steyn in the Free State, South Africa. Petrus Steyn is a small farming town between Tweeling and Kroonstad. Growing up here seemed ideal at the onset because my mother and brother were around. This is important as you will see that I draw some of my positive energy from these two individuals, especially my mother. My mother and brother have always played a key role in my mental and emotional stability. I recall my primary school years where I was confronted and ridiculed for my "soft" demeanour and always reminded that I did not quite fit into the traditional heteronormative constructs of being a boy at the time. People always called me gay and at the time I did not understand what this term meant but I knew that something was off because it was used to mock me, explicitly indicating that I am on the wrong path, I did not fit in and, in some ways, bring shame to my family and the community at large. This was a battle as I did not know how to respond. I knew that some would retaliate with violence, so I just walked away! However, having my brother and mother at the same school was what made school bearable. People knew that my brother would always stand up for me/fight my battles. As for my mother, being a teacher in a small town was and is still considered being in the upper class, and because of this, her position in the community afforded me some privileges in terms of the treatment that I received from both my peers and the community at large. As much as this helped, there were some social spaces where both my mother and brother were not around, and of course this meant I would be abused emotionally by associating me with the derogatory term. Unfortunately, I had to face this torture alone.

This forced me to build a wall or, rather, find alternative ways of protecting myself and this was through finding the right people who would not judge me or engage in conversations pertaining to how the male gender is to be. I chose three girlfriends who would gladly play netball with me and allow me to dress as I pleased. I also chose this one boy who I think knew that our friendship was based on academics. By this I mean, him and I were in an academic symbiotic relationship. We knew the boundaries! I'd only visit him when he was alone at his home or when we had to discuss schoolwork. This was my way of surviving primary school. I had to fight for my sanity and not only rely on my mother and my brother.

My mother believed in my capabilities more than I did and constantly reminded me that I am smart and can solve problems on my own. This started when she would leave me to do my homework alone and go assist my older brother. As much as this used to hurt me at the onset, I began to appreciate the independence. Thinking about it now, I cannot remember a day when she actually sat down with me and guided me through my schoolwork. She always said, "You can do it!" and I thank her for this because today I can go back to these words and know that I would find a solution for myself. I now reflect and see how even choosing friends that would be of benefit to my mental health trace back to this independence. I consciously chose people who would only bring positive energy into my life and intentionally avoided people who ask about this gay persona that I did not know what it meant but made conclusions that it would be a man in a skirt, make-up, hair and nails done lady-like. From this I feared being that person because I knew that deep down this was a person the society did not want around or was constantly ridiculed, and so I avoided this gay persona I was supposedly geared to embody.

High school

Moving to high school, I was now fully conscious of the term "gay". This meant redefining the traditional way of being a man and we now see this from Raewyn Connell's (A scholar working on issues of gender, sexuality and class dynamics) academic work where she speaks about masculinities. By this, Connell refers to the different ways of being a man. I need to clarify this statement. Connell introduced this theory to teach us that there are different ways of being a man and that certain elements "othered" by hegemony are now considered as part of being a man. However, it is still very much contested in South Africa. A recent example is by Nolte Jack who was raped and killed in South Africa on 18 April 2021 by simply expressing his true identity. This is concerning because gay men and women do not feel safe in their communities because of these traditional norms that always gain momentum by men and women mobilising to attack queer lives. Something drastic needs to be done and it is both the responsibility of the government and communities to start this process. As a community, the government has given us a starting point (The Constitution) that we all need to live by. It is up to us now to put this into action. Communities need to stand as one to fight these attacks so as to allow gay men and women to live life as they see fit. We need to begin to have these uncomfortable conversations that will deconstruct ideas of what it means to be normal and consider the after-effects and begin to appreciate the presence of gay men and women. This will also teach children to look beyond gendered roles that are supposed to be assumed by these two binary sexes. I for one knew that I needed to act a certain way to avoid being stigmatised and potentially being harmed as opposed to my primary school years where I now feel my way of dressing, speaking (voice), sports-play (netball) and the friends I kept would put me in jeopardy.

High school was a different ball game. I had to quickly adjust to the heteronormative norm in fear of being judged for my character. This is even more difficult when you go to a high school in your hometown with only black students. These people know you from primary school and have already made up their own minds about your sexuality and will continue to ridicule you. This was my reality!

Later, when my mother decided to move to a high school in Lindley, did I have the opportunity to start afresh. I realised that my first day would determine how I will be treated for the next three years. So, I had to have a game plan and mine was to excel in academics and embody heteronormativity like my life depended on it.

Going to this new town and new school meant adjusting to new ways of discovering my new self. I tried all I could to portray my masculine self by engaging in risky behaviours that would otherwise earn me brownie points from my male friends and buried myself in academics. However, I could not run away from this façade for too long. When I felt that people were onto me, I tried to find new ways I could distil the peace and so, one of the ways I proved this was by dating this girl in Grade 10. The truth is that I only went into the relationship because I wanted her to assist with my façade and it did for some time. The relationship went well with a few naughty touches and kisses but no sex. My excuse was that there was no place we could engage in sexual intercourse because we both lived at boarding school, and both had limited access to each other's building for obvious reasons. So, it was taboo to see either one of us in our respective boarding houses. I maintained this relationship until I told her that I need to focus on school and to my surprise she understood and did not question my decision. But now I had to battle people's opinions of who I am. So later I approached another girl. Honestly, this was tiring as I felt I did not do myself any justice. Any gay man who has ever been in this position will tell you that you are conflicted but choose to entertain this idea. So, each day, I woke and chose this girl and convinced myself that this was the right thing to do as per what was expected of me.

It was only later when I started entertaining this idea of risky behaviour that I found myself with one of the boys in my room after smoking weed. We were kissing and doing all sorts of things but no sex. He just could not penetrate me. It was painful for both of us. The nice thing about this arrangement was that neither of us would be questioned when we were found in bed together. It was considered normal! It was considered a sleepover which was what most boys would be found doing. And not long after that, I was introduced to a pastor who was gay on an app called "Badoo". Myself and this pastor spoke endlessly until we met which is when I enjoyed anal sex. He taught me so much about my own sexuality and to fully express myself. This arrangement carried on until he moved to another town but luckily, I was also moving to Vanderbijlpark, Gauteng in South Africa.

My move to the "Vaal" was to upgrade my matric certificate for university admission. I had applied late to the University of Pretoria. I appreciated being here because my move meant that I had all the freedom in the world to start dating men at my own pace. All I can say about my living in the "Vaal" is that it was an emotional and sexual roller coaster that made me feel liberated most times. I was finding myself at my own pace and would recuperate whenever I felt the need to. Later in the year, I got confirmation from the University of Pretoria to pursue my course the following year.

Moving to Pretoria

In Pretoria, I continued finding myself while focusing on my studies. I knew I only had three years to complete this qualification. Even with all the partying and staying out late, academics were always my priority.

One of the moments I also wish to highlight is being raped. Although this is sometimes hard admitting to myself, I am a rape victim. I have struggled to make sense of this reality for a very long time. However, with time, I have managed to not think about this ordeal and rather refer to myself as a rape survivor. I am a survivor because I have managed to acknowledge the ordeal, to make peace and to know that this experience does not define me or what I stand for. The truth is, minutes after this experience, my friends laughed at me and accused me of a hook-up gone wrong. It becomes difficult to defend oneself to the people close to you; friends at this particular moment when your world is turned upside down. It brings me back to the power of association. I was associated with the wrong people at the wrong time.

One of the things I try to achieve in my life now is restoring peace within my space. I have forgiven myself and others for what has happened to me. Many of the choices I make today are based on these experiences, the lessons and opportunities gained, whether good or bad.

As opposed to years in the "Vaal" and Pretoria, I try to limit my "live in the moment" experiences because I know I do not walk alone. I carry my family, company, and sometimes friends' reputations. No one wants to be associated with an outcast! As a black child, you will know that our parents have always warned us about those children who do not obey their parents' rules and quickly remind us that we will limit our future by associating ourselves with such people. So, I try to be a good boy most times. I escape many things through Netflix and having drinks indoors now.

What's next for Tumi is focusing on his career and actually building a future with somebody's son and trust me, for this somebody's son – there's a criteria! I realised that I need to be kind to myself and so, most of the people I associate myself with bring me a lot of good and show me new strides that I may have not been introduced to.

4
My journey to becoming

Xola Dladla–Nkosi

In very rare cases, people who identify as "straight" never really find themselves in positions where they have to explain their life journey unless they are successful people that want to share relatable stories for the masses as a way of motivation. As queer bodies, we find ourselves in positions to give stories of our upbringing and our current life affairs without being successful business owners or public figures but for merely being ourselves. The goal here is to tell my story and shed some light on my path. How you, as a reader, receive my story is all up to you, so I can only hope that you are motivated to live a life that better serves you.

What being in school meant for me as a gay boy

I grew up in Soweto, a township of the City of Johannesburg Metropolitan Municipality in Gauteng, South Africa, and went to the schools nearby. I was a very outgoing young boy in primary school and very smart when it came to academics. I enrolled in athletics and choir. I was a prefect (what is commonly known as learner's representative council). I suppose being smart and outspoken qualified me to be in that position. I excelled quite well in athletics and became the only athlete in my school to go to national level where I finished in first place. My teachers and I trained every day. I guess being an over achiever in class and in sports disqualified me from being bullied as a gay boy. I don't think at the time I understood my position in society, I just knew that I liked boys. I would write love letters to straight boys and we would be in relationships and it was quite normal. Thinking about this now makes me aware that as children we just follow our hearts and never really pay attention to what the society has to say about being gay or straight. I dated about seven boys in my primary school and the whole school knew but thought nothing of it. It only became problematic in Grade 6 when people started to see me differently. I think they saw a gay person before they saw a star athlete or top academic achiever. I was described as "the gay one", even by my Mathematics teacher. My Life Orientation teacher never understood me. She forced me to stop hanging out with girls and pushed me to play soccer with the boys. It was a different time for me, I didn't know what was going on and I thought I'm going through changes. So, I stuck with soccer, I played it even when I was home. I even played with a local soccer team. At this point I was very aware of myself and who I was. All my titles were stripped from me and all they could see was *I-Stabane*, as they would call me. I got onto the team trying to prove that I'm not what they say I am. I kissed a girl to prove a point and told my stepdad that I love girls. Eventually, I stopped playing soccer. I quit playing with boys and went back to doing all the things I enjoyed doing. My mother knew all of this but I assume she didn't know what to say to me at the time. I also never found myself in a position where I needed to "come out", because she always supported me. I graduated my primary school and went to middle school which was from Grade 7 to 9.

It was a new school. Most of us came from the same primary school but we still met a lot of new people. To me this was liberating because I had a point to prove – to myself and to all those around me. I set goals to become the school president, to be the best athlete and to be the best singer in the choir. I became all those things. I was the best athlete the school ever had, I was school president in Grade 9 and at the end of every end of term the school would announce the top five students from each class. I was in the top five every term for three years. I sang alto in choir and I was the only boy singing in a female voice group. I had a solo song that I sang in the school choir competition. I had achieved every goal that I set when I went to that school and every teacher loved me. With all the positions I occupied in that school, I still chose to be very true to myself. I was very aware that I identify as gay. Even being the smartest kid, I was still bullied verbally. But I never cared because even through those hurdles I knew some people still adored me and liked me for being gay. Most of all, I really loved myself. I still dated boys that identified as straight, but only in private. All my relationships were private, not because I wanted them to be like that but because the boys I dated wanted to keep it a secret.

What qualified people to call me gay was because of my mannerisms, how I spoke, how I acted, who I hung out with and how neat I was, strange as that is. I had two other gay friends in middle school and we were each other's support systems. We would talk about boys and talk about who got a boner from looking at who – they were like my human diary. We spent all our time together, even outside school.

My mother supported everything I did and just knew who I was without questioning it. Some family members would feel the need to point out that I'm gay but my dad, my grandmother and my mom stood up for me. My parents were never together so I would visit my dad during school holidays, and we had the best times together. I hung out with all my cousins and it was normal. I was never made to feel different or treated differently unless the word "gay" was said in between arguments as kids.

My upbringing, in my opinion, was like any other normal child. I think I made it easier for my family by just being myself. I never felt the need to hide how I behaved. I guess I was never really in control of that. However, I would only wear my mother's heels in private, and my grandmother's wigs and a lot of mascara when no one was home. I did all these things in private and only showed a normal boy version of myself to the family. So even through being accepted; I still kept parts of me hidden.

Grades 10 to 12, I still had the same issues of being called names but I just never cared at that point. I was smart and I wanted all that to come through for itself. I think being smart kept me strong because I had a point to prove – I am more than what my gender is to the rest of the society. Being the best singer in school and my participation in a professional all girls dance crew proved that I was capable of things that were never thought to be a possibility for a gay person. I was an athlete as well in high school and was in charge of extra mural activities. I WAS ALL THAT even through the everyday struggles of being constantly reminded that I'm gay.

I never felt the urge to be anyone else but myself and I think that scared people. I saw a lot of gay people change themselves to avoid being bullied or called names. I was hated by gay people because I never changed for anyone and they felt like I was the reason straight people hate us.

Getting into the first real relationship

I first had my real relationship with a gay person when I was 16 and he was 23 at the time. I never knew about anal sex or how gay people have sex until I met him. I didn't know that I identified as "bottom" until he explained it to me. Even worse was that I didn't know that one had to clean themselves before having sex. I assume he thought I knew. Luckily for us both, nothing strange happened. But, I remember being so worried about engaging in sex. It took me an hour to calm down before he could even penetrate me. I was just nervous. He was very understanding and allowed me to relax. I loved that he respected me and didn't push me to do things I didn't want to do unless I was ready.

He was a dancer as well, in a popular male group and he knew of me because I was in the famous female dance crew. I guess I was famous because I was the only boy in that crew, so everybody wanted to see me dance. We were at a competition once and his crew was there, and our crew was there and we had very strict dance instructors so they never allowed us to see other dancers until the competition was over. We met that day and started dating a week later. I still smile when remembering how I felt when I first met him. We dated until I was 19. We went our separate ways because we grew apart.

I was Somizi's dancer, a South African media personality, television presenter, actor and choreographer; by the time I was 19 and I was travelling a lot. So I had no time for anything else but dance. In 2016, I went on tour with Joyous Celebration, a South African gospel group and I was on the road for the whole year. I had no relationships during this time.

Going into University

In 2017, I enrolled at the University of Witwatersrand. This was a big moment for me as I was in a new place altogether. I had five of my friends from high school with me so it was easier navigating varsity life together as first years. It was both the best and the scariest experience I've had, but I think I have always been an agent of change. This is a place where the person who was only wearing heels and make up in private and for dance shows came out during the day and did all those things that I was so afraid to do growing up. This is the place where I grew in so many ways. I understood my purpose in life and I felt a sense of freedom. Nobody cared what I wore, what I looked like or how I identified; everybody just wanted to hang out and have fun. For me this was part of my enlightenment. It proved that a person can only grow outside of their comfort zone. Nobody cared that I was smart, the best dancer, the best singer or gay. I was no longer a person because of my titles or my position in society. I was me, nothing else, and that gave me room to grow and taught me to stop investing myself in how other people see me but invest myself in being the best version of me.

I am still evolving every day; I learn my strengths every day and I survive through my failures. I stopped looking for the validation to know that I matter. I have an important role to play in society. I have stopped letting people's ideas and fears narrate my own journey when I have the paper and the pen to write my own story and live for me and for all those that look like me.

I am holding on because...

God is my home. He is my best friend. He's both my mother and my father, my partner, my boyfriend and my therapist.

In a nutshell, he is my everything. He keeps me sane and keeps me going and provides me with a sense of peace that I cannot put into words. Despite what the church says about homosexuality, I think our purpose on earth is more than what people say it is. My one wish for all my people is to look inside themselves and find that God lies within. The bible even says "greater is he who lives inside of me than the one who lives in the world". He saves, he heals, he restores, he supports us in all that we do and, most of all, he loves unconditionally. I want my people to know that we are more than just *FABULOUS* which is associated with flamboyance. We are successful business owners, philanthropists, narrators of destinies, teachers of the world, pastors and ministers, successful artists and we are worthy of love, marriage, successful careers and a life worth living. Nothing is a mistake, no one is a mistake, even if we are born in conflict and our lives carry too much pain; we are more than that. Wherever you are now reading this, know that you are bigger than whichever struggle/battle you may be facing, and you will come out of it only if you believe you can; only if you believe that God has a plan for you. God is there with you, loving you and guiding you, he will never give up on you for anybody. We are of God. We were created in his image, and we know he never makes mistakes. So, rest in your purpose knowing that your life is a blessing to you and your family.

5
The Brotherhood

Obakeng Pholo

How did I get here? Those words kept ringing in my head as I sat and watched a Beyonce concert in a room full of gay men. It had a mattress on the floor, the lights were off and weed smoke created a fog-like a cloud that enveloped all of us and together with an intense smell of lubricant and alcohol they created an intoxicating atmosphere that was crippling enough to make leaving seem like a harder task than it should be. I think just basking in its comfort seemed like the easier option yet being part of this moment, I knew I should feel some type of shame. Shame that I am a part of a thing I knew I could never talk about but all I felt was happiness – I felt a sense of belonging and comfort I have rarely felt in my life.

My life at home

I had what most people would consider a fairly good upbringing. I had my mom, my dad, and sisters. My parents worked low-skilled jobs but still, they worked. We had God, who made life bearable. I am not sure exactly when things started to take a turn. However, growing up gay in a township can very quickly start to feel like you are a fish that is washed out of the sea and you lying there on the sand hoping the tide comes close enough to get you before it is too late.

For a long time, I felt like an outsider, especially in a small township in the middle of nowhere where gay culture practically didn't exist. I had friends and they loved me as much as teenagers can love each other. However, I was the only boy amongst girls, and I learnt quickly that I wasn't a boy who could hang out with other boys. They would be uncomfortable around me or would make jokes about the fact that I was a boy who behaved like a girl.

Teenagers tend to be indifferent about people who are different from them. That indifference turned into bullying for me. The bullying happened as I was transitioning from primary school into high school. As an outsider, I had to find companionship elsewhere and that became books and television. I would go into my friend's homes and ask to borrow a book that I had seen on the table or somewhere in their homes. I guess the bullying was a blessing in some way because I soon started to excel academically which made most of bullies more eager to be my friend than to beat me up.

The experience of being bullied can be traumatising, some people hardly ever mentally recover from the experience. My experience of being bullied was funny in a sad way. I think psychologists might categorise my experience as Stockholm syndrome. My first crush was my main bully. A dark-skinned, well-built, athletic boy from my class. I still am not sure what could have led to those types of feelings, but I think now, looking back, that it might have been a combination of things: constant attention from a male and this longing I have always had to be needed. He needed me academically and financially and that made me feel like I was the most important person in his life. Plus, on top of everything else, he was a very good-looking boy.

Once the transition into high school had happened, the bullying stopped completely, but nothing prepares you for the teenage years. The rush of emotions amplified every experience. My feminine side was visible to everyone, even strangers, which made me an easy target for a lot of things. Sexual abuse of boys who look and acted like me is very high in townships and has become a secret we all know about, but we never address it with the seriousness that such a subject requires.

I remember telling my first gay friend about the incident that happened to me when I was 15 years old with an older guy in my neighbourhood and all he said was "Oh it happened to me too". We both just sat there in silence for a while and moved on to talking about what we were going to eat and never spoke about it again. Sexual abuse at a young age often leads to unhealthy love relationships, unwanted sexual desires, and really deep scars.

When you are part of the gay community, it seems like you are guaranteed that a lot of bad things that could possibly happen to a human being will definitely happen to you. Rejection by society is a big part of growing up gay but I think the most painful rejection is rejection by your family. I could never really imagine how it feels not to be accepted by your own parent. I have been lucky that I never had to come out. My family knew from my behaviour that I was gay and so they had no real expectation of me being anything else but gay. In all that chaos of my life, I found religion. It happened during my teenage years. Most children in townships are raised in the church in some way. God for me represented a gateway to all that was good in the world, everything that the world needed. Sundays remain my favourite day of the week. It is when people usually bring out their best selves, well back in the early 2000s that is, I don't see it anymore.

It took a while, but I eventually learnt the church had a lot of issues. There was a hidden culture of hate, lust, greed, lies, and just pure evil masquerading as the holy spirit. I started to realise that religion was being used as weapons to chastise, discriminate, isolate, and punish those that did not abide by its rules. Reading up on the history of religion, I have been shocked at how such an institution that had invited so much peace into my life could be responsible for so much damage in the world.

Despite everything, my belief in God remains. Maybe I have found a way to separate God from religion. My belief in God has not stopped anything bad from happening, yet I believe that God is constantly cheering me on, helping me when it is necessary and protecting me at all times. So, I believe even when things were absolutely terrible and they have been, I always knew they could have been worse.

My late teenage years became even harder; I don't think it would have mattered what my sexuality was. I think the teenage years are hard for everyone. It doesn't matter what sexuality or race you are or what privileges you may have in life, the raging hormones that come with being that age can sometimes be too much. I have attempted to take my life at least twice. My first attempt was at 14; I had written what was supposed to be my suicide letter to my mother, and in that letter, I had talked about how hard it has been for me and how she has been a great mother. I told her that I don't want to be gay.

I saw that the only way out of this life was death. Being gay brought me so much pain so early on in life. I didn't see how I could survive to grow old like this. The rate of suicide for gay people is, apparently, very high. I am not sure where I got this, but suicide is said to be the second leading cause of death. I assumed that HIV was the first and being murdered was the third one suggesting that even if I didn't succeed at killing myself, chances are high that someone else might do it anyway.

Death at times seems like the easiest way out for most people in my community. Dealing with being a human and being gay can break some people. Our lives seem to be dedicated to surviving! Surviving the bullying and exclusion as a child, surviving the corrective rape incidents and emotional trauma as teenagers, surviving feelings of loneliness and depression as young adults and surviving feelings of being unwanted all our lives.

Yet, the gay community has always been full of resilient people. We work hard and hope for all the things that everyone else seems to get freely. Love and affection were two of the things I prayed for all my life. So, I knew that the liberation of leaving that small township in the middle of nowhere was the answer to all my prayers so I worked as hard as I could to leave, and I did.

Moving out...

The first year of college opened my eyes to a whole world of possibilities. It helped me realise that the fairytale won't suddenly happen just because I left the township and that there are many years of hard work still ahead of me. Before I left for college, I wanted to pursue a career in education or health. I didn't qualify to enrol in any of the schools or courses I wanted. I was sad for most of my first year.

Mental health is something our generation is still trying to understand. We can now make the distinction between depression and grief and other mental health issues like trauma. I now know that what I was experiencing was grief, grief over a catastrophic loss of a family member and grief over a life I had dreamt about for a long time. For almost a year, I went through days and nights of wishing for death. I would walk down the street and think if I walk slow enough while crossing the robots, maybe those cars would hit me, and I would die. I was lucky enough that the experience was short-lived. It also didn't require any medical intervention.

Even though I have always wanted love, getting into a relationship seemed like something that would never happen. I went on one of those dating apps that turned into a hook-up app like most of those apps usually do. I had no expectation of love, maybe a date or casual hook-ups but nothing romantic. Well, to my surprise I met a beautiful man who I could only describe now as my kingdom come.

I won't try to paint my first love experience as this big fairy tale. It was gentle, playful and beautiful, he was out of my league, and I loved him but the experience unearthed a lot of my insecurities. I was very young, we both were which is not meant to be an excuse, and my ideas of love and romance were very limited to what I had read and what I had seen on TV. I guess for the most part that is what I wanted and really fought for – a picture-perfect relationship with date nights, walks and cuddling all the time. I soon realised there was still too much self-love I needed to do and unlearning unrealistic ideas of love.

Romance between two people is often messy and complicated. The romance between two men with no real-life examples of their type of relationship can be difficult. Firstly, coming from a background where healthy love relationships hardly exist and, secondly, where gay love relationships were never even thought to exist makes it even more complicated. I walked into my first relationship with a heteronormative idea of a relationship. I was the girl, and he was the guy, everything had to play out in that scenario. I have seen a lot of people carry that idea into their relationships.

Almost two years after entering my first relationship, it ended. Nobody ever tells you that there is emotional pain that can feel like it is taking physical form. It felt like my heart was being run over by a truck over and over and nothing could stop it. I have become more sympathetic to stories I hear of people taking their own lives because of a breakup. The pain was worse than anything I have ever felt before.

I think my breakup was the final straw in a list of painful things. I vowed from that day that I would never allow myself to feel that way ever again or to allow myself to be in such a situation of someone having so much power over me. My insecurities followed me outside the relationship, I constantly felt fat and being in a new environment didn't help even though it had been a few of years since having left home.

Sex education

The decision to join the gym gave rise to my sexual liberation. Hooking up with random men made me feel like I was finally in charge of my sexuality, my sexual desires, and my emotions. Whenever I needed to feel good about myself, I would go on an app and meet a nice random stranger to help me feel good about myself. These strangers often didn't care much about my weight, height, or financial background – they were horny, I was horny and that is all it was, an exchange and that is where it ended.

Of course, with sexual liberation comes risky behaviour. We often cannot talk about being gay and not at some point talk about HIV. It has become such a big part of our lives for a long time that being gay and being HIV positive were intertwined. Learning about sexual health like condoms, PreP, and ARVs really started sinking in much later in my life since I really had no real healthy sexual experiences and never thought it would be something that I would need to know. Again, there is no real gay sex education that is freely available in townships.

There are terms in the gay community to help us understand sexual preferences that also came to me at a late stage in my life – being asked if I am top, bottom or versatile still makes me uncomfortable at times. When I started realising I was bottom, I felt a little shame. The question would be asked, and the answer would be met with a lot of disappointment like I had done something wrong. I later learnt about bottom shaming; that being penetrated somehow made you a little less manly, which is funny because we both men. The chances that we will want to have penetrative sex at some point are high, and how do they think that is going to happen if they constantly look down on bottoms?

Being the bottom means I stand a higher risk of contracting HIV and STIs. Learning this fact came much later than it should have. I learnt about cleanliness when having sex through a friend who, after I had a bad hook-up, explained to me that I can prevent such things with a better diet and douching. Making sure I was clean before my sexual escapades really did give me confidence, way too much confidence.

Contracting an STI brought me back to my senses. I had mucus coming out of my anus and it caused issues with my ability to go to the bathroom. The scariest part was not the STI, it was people finding out I had an STI. I quietly went to a clinic, got shots of penicillin and antibiotics and remembered my favourite line, "it could have been worse".

Sexual liberation has brought with it a tendency of risky behaviour. There is still a lot of stigma around sexually liberated individuals. There are really bad words that are often used to shame sexual liberation. As much as we, in our circles, can talk about orgies, threesomes and all types of sexual experiences that we have had, nobody ever makes it a healthy conversation.

I have never been fat enough to be considered fat, nor skinny enough to be called slender. I could be regarded as chubby or thick depending on the day. Since I was going to the gym, I could deal with those comments about my weight, but my femininity started becoming an issue as I was dealing with the weight. The question: "are you straight acting?" would constantly show up during conversations on dating apps. I am not feminine enough to be considered a fem bottom but again I am not masculine enough to be regarded as straight acting so all the answers I gave felt like a lie.

Masculinity and femininity are a big thing for gay people. Being feminine is considered being too gay and nobody likes gays who are too gay. It is like there is a limitation on how gay you can be and once you pass that point, you are out. Straight acting guys or masculine guys are celebrated, and a preference for real men is often shouted out the loudest in gay groups. We all do it from time to time, even go as far as complaining about how the too gay guys set us back. We are still in the process of acceptance of ourselves as gay people and understanding internalised homophobia in our own community.

I have never understood why feminine energy posed such a threat to society, whenever feminine energy shows up it is always told to dim its light. Feminine energy can often get you into trouble especially if you are considered a "man". You are labelled as weak. The older I become, the more I wonder if my feminine energy was the reason I was bullied, was raped and why I have been side lined in conversations. It even happens to straight women; just being a woman in society is a danger.

I am still pondering on the idea of if I had a high sex drive or a sex addiction in my early 20s. I have seen a lot of gay men fall into many addictions. Alcohol and sex are the most popular ones and, like overeating, the black community celebrates over drinking and men celebrate an unhealthy attachment to sex so often the lines are blurred where the distinction cannot be made if this is a serious problem that needs attention or just over enjoyment.

Addictions are an escape from reality. A way to make yourself happy even if it is just for a few minutes, a way to feel anything else but the bad feelings. When I started out in college, I still recall a number of fresh-faced first years who were eager to start a new life but over the years, I have seen a lot of them succumb to HIV, and alcohol abuse destroying their lives. I have heard stories of drug addiction turning people into kleptomaniacs.

The party scene is amazing, friendship circles are amazing. This is how we have built our own little communities, and the families we choose. But all too often we lose ourselves in those lives. We lose ourselves in the hype, impressing friends, and engaging in risky behaviour. Maybe it's because we are seeking the things that make this life a little more bearable. Maybe waiting for that big hoopla that never comes is the reason we eventually end up here with a group of gay men all sitting together seeking some type of redemption from the mess that is life.

Conclusion

Looking across this room right now, thinking about the life I have lived and the amazing men sitting here in their state of undress, I see excellence. I see the boys who fought to get out of townships and villages across this country to come here and pursue a better life. I know the city is not the only place that this better life can be achieved. Many are changing mindsets about gay culture in the villages and townships we ran away from, and we are grateful for them. Our paths are different, mine led me to this city so I can be able to tell these types of stories.

So, sitting here, I will not allow myself to feel shame about this experience or any other experience that I have had. Life has been painful and difficult, but it has also been beautiful. Looking back now, I realise that I would never change a thing. I realise this is how we find community in each other, and even though we never really talk about it, our shared life experiences are what brought us all here, to seek healing in each other and brotherhood. We have all been victims at some point and we have all felt side lined in our own communities by our own families. My story is not unique; there are some parts I could never talk about, some parts that were too painful to ever revisit but sometimes I pick through that window and realise, I have survived.

6

Mommy Knows,
So Who Cares?

Lerato Mofokeng

One of my friends asked who was the one person who has kept me together all these years; I responded with "my mother". So, I decided to reflect on my journey I shared with her and, in a way, pay tribute to her. I have noted that this black skin and sexual orientation is not seen for its beauty, potential and contribution but as a disruption to the so-called patriarchal society. To be able to effectively contribute; I have decided to deliberately disrupt.

My decision to disrupt was inspired by a conversation I had with my mother when I was coming out to her and she offered comforting remarks, reassuring me of my existence and her support. Allow me now to take you through a shortened version of my story with a selection of short-illustrative narratives from what I regard as critical moments. After deep reflections of these life-defining moments, it has become clear to me why and how I have become who I am today.

Narrative moments

Since each of us are unique, some people might say friends, romantic relationship, or money, for example, are what they need to survive. I believe that I could not have lived without my family. Although people may face discrimination for a variety of reasons, discrimination based solely on sexual orientation is unmatched. I was really hurt by it, especially when I was young. I simply did not get why I was not like other boys and why I was not eager to play with other boys.

I used to be the timid boy, with a soft or weird voice and I would find comfort around girls, playing skipping or with girl toys. I don't know where I learnt to make clothes, but my doll had a lot of outfits. I had to make a plan. I used to be teased a lot for being myself by other children. As you know, children can be bullies but I just cried and sucked it up.

Heading for high school, I felt that this "thing" that makes me different from other boys was getting worse. I used to dread lunchtimes and going to school since there were no boys I could relate to. Instead, they would all be playing soccer, leaving me to sit by myself or hang out with a group of girls but I would get bullied for doing that. This made me feel really sad both inside and outside of class so much so that I couldn't wait for the bell to ring at the end of the last period so I could go home and unwind after a hard day of misery. This had a terrible impact on my academic life. I used to be shy in class and would often hesitate to ask the teacher a question when I didn't understand anything. I developed the habit of hiding behind my voice and always wished to go undetected and unbothered by teachers or my schoolmates. I would simply go to school, go home, and repeat the process the following day. It had become a habit.

This isolation even caused me to fail Grade 9. This was the most difficult time in my life as I was most affected by my sexuality. I didn't like being different. I asked God. Why me? The worst was that my family made me take science classes despite the fact that they knew I struggled with mathematics. They believed that engineers and other persons in math and science-related professions were the only ones who succeeded in life in terms of landing the best positions and earning good salaries.

Yes, it would have been great to have studied along that career path, but since we are all different in our ways of being, we cannot all have the same passions. However, if you gave me a chart and a pencil, I could draw anything. I am artistic. I was usually the kid who didn't complete his homework, missed class, and had the worst grades. I frequently reflect on how my life would have turned out if I had known what was going on (about my sexuality). I wish someone had talked to me or explained everything to me and told me that being different and being your authentic self is good in its own way.

I wish I could have read a book that had coping mechanisms for LGBTIQ+ teenagers. Maybe if I had accepted myself back then, I would have had the self-assurance and fortitude to handle the issues I was faced with. Maybe if I didn't care about what people thought of me, I might have participated in public speaking or joined the debate team, and maybe I would have been more inspired to go to school, participate, and do well. Obviously, I would advance in life if I had good marks. Since my friends didn't have to go through what I went through, they were able to excel in school, stuck with their studies, and find solace in being top students.

Now that I'm in university, we all dress however we choose. Now that I know what I want – I like boys – I can't do anything to change it and nothing will change it. At this point in my life, I no longer care what other people think of me and there is no longer any bullying because we are all adults. Around 2014 and 2015, I experienced a rebirth. I was beginning to accept my sexuality and could choose to spend time with whoever I wanted without fear of condemnation.

Meeting someone I thought or still think is the love of my life.

One day, I met a boy by the name of Lesego. The name I have used is fictious but Lesego represents someone I was in a romantic relationship with. He completely floored me. I had made the decision to spend the rest of my life with him as soon as I laid eyes on him. We chose to go on dates. I've never experienced such extremes of pleasure and misery in my life. I made the decision to come out to my family and everyone else in my life after dating him for just one month. I told my mum that I was gay and she embraced me. It felt so good to post "love lives here" pictures on social media. It's the controversy that was so exciting, people were shocked that I am gay.

Lesego was based in Johannesburg at the time, and I stayed with my mother and sister in Sebokeng, a middle-class township in southern Gauteng, South Africa near the industrial cities of Vanderbijlpark and Vereeniging . The distance between the two places was approximately an hour's travel by taxi. Every time he invited me over to his place, it was impossible to travel back home, so I would sleep over. This used to cause so much tension between my mom and I. She was not strict but didn't approve of me just sleeping over at my friends without her permission. She asked my sister to speak to me about my behaviour. The following day, my sister spoke to me regarding this and without any fear I said, you know I am not a problematic child, it's just that I am in a relationship now and I have to make time for my partner. We have limited time. We spend enough time if I sleep over. I told her that the person I am dating is a boy; I am gay! He is wonderful and handsome. My sister was not surprised, she just said "okay, I understand, I've always known that you are gay but please do not tell mom about this, it would kill her to find out about your sexuality". She suggested that I just continue with my things under the carpet and maybe come out to my mom later when I am no longer under her roof. I tried to do that but my relationship with my mom was becoming compromised. I had to put an end to it. So I started planning how am I going to let her know that the person I am with is my boyfriend. I had to tell her so that she can know and give me permission to visit my "bae" without that causing commotion and unnecessary conflicts in the house. The distance between Lesego and I contributed to me coming out sooner than I wanted to. It was damage control.

On a boring weekday, my mother and I were just having a conversation and she was telling me that one of her friends does not want to accept her son's girlfriend because the girlfriend is older than her son. She went on and on about how she would never do that to me. She told me that she loves me so much that she would accept any kind of woman that I am in love with. She knows exactly how it feels to have your mother-in law not like you – she went through the same predicament. I realised that this is the perfect time to talk about my situation.

I asked her "so if you are saying you would accept anyone I bring home, would the same apply if I bring a boy?"

For a moment she startled and was confused by my statement, I repeated the question again. In shock and disappointment her reply was: "Are you gay". I said, "yes, yes I am gay; since you love me so much, would you please accept that I am gay. I have found someone. That's the reason I have been sleeping out sometimes". "I never meant to hurt you" I said; "I just wanted to clear the air". I told her that I know it is a disappointment, that I had gone to war with myself regarding this, and that I tried to fight it. I started crying! I tried to change, to supress my feelings and praying about it, I just cannot change it. I did not choose this! I was born this way.

She started crying too, and said "baby it's okay, there is no dustbin where we can throw our children because they are gay. I carried you for nine months and I gave birth to you, I love you unconditionally. So tell me about this boy that you are seeing", and I did. "He sounds like a good boy and it seems like he makes you happy, I don't mind" she replied. "As long as he will love you and protect you from any harm. Just protect yourself" she said. I think it was an indirect way of saying please use condoms to protect yourself from diseases, but you know our African parents, they are not comfortable discussing sex with their children.

After that conversation, I felt as if some sort of burden was lifted off my shoulders. It felt like the burden I have been carrying all these years was all gone, taken away. What a relief! Whoever reading this and has not disclosed their sexuality to their parents, I strongly recommend that you do this. I promise you it's going to be the best day of your life. Home will suddenly feel like home; that's if your parents and your family will react like my mom did. She just gave me a long teddy bear hug and assured me that it's okay and I am loved regardless.

I brought Lesego home a week after that and my family loved him. I think my father was the one who was more disappointed, but he came to terms with it. Years passed and now we are here, but unfortunately things did not work out as

I had planned with Lesego. We dated for four years. I think he is my soul mate, but I will love him from a distance. Ever since I came out at home, I didn't care who was unfairly treating me or gossiping about me or teasing me about my sexuality. My family knows. The most important person in my life, my mother, knows, supports me and loves me the way I am. I really don't care what people say; my family are accepting and this greatly helped me to accept myself.

The tragedy – November 2020

In November 2020, my mom and her friends had gone on a trip to Durban. They were entrepreneurs. My mom used to sell shoes, bags, umbrellas, all sorts of things. I think I get my entrepreneurship passion from her. She was a single mother and provided everything we needed through this kind of income. She has never worked a day in her life for anyone but there was nothing I ever wanted for. We never went to bed on an empty stomach. So she, together with her friends, went to a factory in Durban to go buy stock of the items that they sell. They travelled in a minibus.

I remember receiving a call saying that my mother was involved in an accident. Two huge tucks crashed into the minibus on a highway on their way back home. All thirteen of them including the driver died. We quickly had to rush to go identify their bodies and come back with them. Some bodies were unidentifiable. I am still devastated; that picture of seeing my mom in pieces is still in my head. A part of me died that day. I lost everything!

I feel like I am alone without my mother. Yes, I love the people in my life, but I don't really find comfort from them. I pray that this emptiness will end one day and that I will feel whole again. I have always wanted to have children – two to be exact – I am hoping for a boy and a girl. I have a feeling that when God blesses me with a child that maybe it will fill that void that I have now in my heart from losing the most important person in my life by replacing it with another that will be so dear to my heart. I am also wishing for a great companionship one day with a loving and peaceful partner who will always be there to listen, to give me hugs, kisses, and tell me everything is going to be alright; that he will always be there for me and will help me get through this grief.

The road ahead

From this moment on, I am going to live my life to the fullest; the way my mother would have wanted. She was an advocate for my education. That's all she begged me to do; to be educated so that I can take myself out of the township and poverty. I strongly believe that I gained myself a powerful and protective angel. There is no way that I will not succeed in anything I start. I am studying law. Completing my degree and practicing is one of my goals that I have set for myself. I am also trying to start a business. I have a lot of ideas, no capital whatsoever, but I will make a plan like my mommy always did. I will not stay in a place of pain for years. I need to move. The camera is still rolling, remember I am a creative, fate and the universe will direct me into the arts, TV and fashion.

What you can take from this, is that life is too short! You do not have all the time that you think you have. Either you will die very soon, or your loved ones are going to leave you. With the 1-minute remaining, be honest with yourself, accept yourself, love yourself, and take care of yourself. Dream, do not touch the ground, fight, laugh, run, and stand your ground for what you believe in. We spend so much of our time worrying about what people are going to say or think about us instead of using that energy to develop ourselves and better our lives. Whether you do good or you do bad, they will always talk.

7
Breathe

Olebogeng Seripe

Growing up as the youngest of seven kids in an African religious family that believed in God and education more than anything else was not easy. To people from the outside, it looked like my siblings and I grew up with silver spoons in our mouths just because our parents were civil servants. I grew up in a family where it was the parents way or the highway. My dad often used to say, "Jacob is the President of South Africa and he controls South Africa; I am the president of this house and I control this house". My parents were like dictators, and they dictated what we wore, who we hung out with and where we hung out. Children in my family were not allowed to speak unless they were spoken to. Disagreeing with my parents was the highest level of disrespect according to them. However, they meant well.

My father was a school principal and church elder in a reformed church. He was well respected and well known in the community. He always had good reputation and was a people's person. My mom was a nurse at a hospital nearby and just an ordinary Methodist church member until she got offended and we started church hopping which eventually led us into a Pentecostal/ charismatic church where she gained a position at the church and that's when she started behaving like we live in heaven. She was a bit of a bossy boots and always wanted to get things right. She loved helping other people and sometimes she would put strangers needs before her own family's needs because she believed that God called her to help others. She was one of the Good Samaritans of our community.

My journey

I grew up in a small community where everyone knew each other, and they also knew everything about everyone. The community was so small that we were all neighbours. We knew each other by names and family names. So, I was known as "Olebogeng *wa* Seripe *wa tichere/nurse*". This means that they referred to me by surname and my parents' professions and because of that I had to make sure that whatever I do does not give my parents or family a bad reputation. I had to be careful of what I said in the streets or at school, how I acted and how I played with other children. This had a huge impact on me as a child because of the amount of pressure it put on me.

I was a humble and loveable child. Most elders were fond of me because I was very respectful. At school I was a teachers' pet, loved by all teachers not only because of my manners but because I was one of the top achievers throughout primary school. I was always neat and tidy, and homework was always done and submitted on time. However, all this affected me and who I was a child.

I was about 4 years old when I realised that I was different. I didn't know how different I was or why was I different from other boys. It was at this age when I realised that I was attracted to other boys. Every time my friends and I play "house", be it at creche or at home, I would always choose to be the sister or the girl from next door. I never wanted to be a male character because that would ruin my chances of dating other boys. From time to time, I would ask my mom why I was a boy instead of a girl and she would jokingly tell me that I was born a girl and she prayed to God to change my gender because she wanted a boy. For a very long time, I believed her, but I was confused and angry at her because all I wanted was to be a girl like my best friend, Tshepang.

My family knew that I was different. They loved me as I was and to some extent, they embraced who I was as a child, they were very supportive and never once did they judge me. My mom was my number one supporter. She would buy me Bratz dolls and all the pretty things little girls wanted instead of cars, guns and other toys that were for "boys" only. She would let my best friend and I play dress up with her clothes because she knew that made me happy. My mom understood that I hated sports, especially soccer, with all my heart. Every time my dad or teachers at school would force me to play soccer, she would come to my defence. She would tell them that she doesn't want me to have scars and get injured because boys are rough in nature. The more she came to my defence, the more comfortable I became because I knew that I had someone in my corner.

At pre-school, during playtime I would make sure that I was the first person at the toy room so that I could choose the best "girl toys" and props so I can be the hottest girl. This was all in the name of fun. At that time, I still didn't understand what was going on with me, but I enjoyed every bit of it. During nap time, I always made sure that I slept next to the cutest boy/s so that I could feel special, and again it was all fun and games. From time to time, I would compete with the girls in my class about who hangs out with the cutest boys in our class, and I'd end up winning. And that's how I became friends with girls.

In 2006, I started my first grade in a local multiracial school. It was a combined school starting at Grade 1 and finishing at Grade 9. Adjusting and adapting to the school was easy because most of the children from our pre-school went to the same school and it was as if we were continuing onto the next grade. It was less of a new beginning and more of a continuation. That was a blessing in disguise because I was a very shy kid and I found it difficult to make new friends. I still do.

Months went by and slowly but surely the new school started to become hell for me and other boys that were like me – those that preferred playing with girls and playing with dolls. The older learners started calling us names. At first, they referred to me as *spharela banyana* which means a [boy] who is always sitting with girls and later on I became known as *sphare* to my classmates and everyone else in the school. At that time,

I wasn't bothered by the name *sphare*; I had bigger problems to worry about such as the ugly heavy "Bronx" school shoes that my mom bought for me because they were strong and were supposed to last me for a long time.

Two years later, my parents decided that I had to change schools because it was alleged that there was forgery of the learners' end year results by the school principal. I went to a new local school where I was not acquainted with everyone there. It was a new environment which means that it came with different kind of problems. The bullying was more intense, it was more physical than just name calling. And because of that, I had to make sure that the bullies would not be able to tell that I am a softie who crushes on other boys. I did not know anyone at that school so it meant that I had to find something to hide behind and something that will make me acceptable.

I chose religion and academics as my masks. I hid behind religion; it was my excuse for not wanting to kiss girls. On Fridays during break time, all the learners would gather at the assembly point, and we would play indigenous games. One of which was, *tie ya bapala* which is a game played by boys and girls where they would stand in a circle and whoever is chosen by the group as the first player would go around the circle with a tie and choose a boy or a girl to kiss. They would put a tie around the neck of whoever they choose and kiss them until they feel like stopping and then the person who was kissed becomes the second player and does the same thing. The aim of the game was that girls would kiss their crushes or boys would try to kiss the prettiest girls. Poor me could not play the game because I would be forced to kiss girls and all I wanted was to kiss another boy, but I couldn't do that or else I would risk being bullied for the rest of my primary school years and possibly get into trouble and end up in the principal's office and be accused of bringing demons to the school. That was the risk I couldn't take.

I spent all my primary school years hiding behind being a cheese boy who comes from a religious family. Although I did date girls, I would not kiss them because I was not attracted to them. This, however, did not stop me from being attracted to boys. Every now and then during free periods, the older boys in our class would sit in the corner and start talking about their body changes due to puberty and some of them would talk about their sexual experiences. I would always find myself intrigued by the topic, although I would not have anything to add to the conversation. I would sit there and fantasise, embarrassingly so, about me and other boys doing what they were taking about. If the topic was about body changes, I would quietly sit there and wish that one of the boys would invite me over to their houses for a sleep over so I would get to see those body changes as well.

However, instead of expressing how I felt at that time, I became more curious each day. I ended up asking my neighbour to download "mxit" for me without my parents being aware because they hated "mxit" and believed that one can become demon possessed from chatting with strangers on the internet. After setting up my profile, I began to catfish boys. I pretended to be a girl and started dating boys on "mxit" and that felt good but also made me more and more curious which led to my discovery of gay porn.

Discovering gay porn and being able to save the videos and pictures on my phone was a seal for me. That was the confirmation that I was not only physically attracted to boys, but I was sexually attracted to them as well. I wanted to explore and experiment. However, I could not because the more I became curious was the more I became religious. My two favourite things to search on the internet became XXX videos and bible scriptures about homosexuality.

I still didn't understand anything about sexuality. All I knew was that I was curious, and I had to pray the curiosity away or I would end up going to hell. This led me to spending most of my high school years miserable, confused and emotionally drained because I had to live two different lives. On the internet, I was dating boys and I was into boys but in real life I was dating girls. At this time, I had convinced myself that it was just a phase that I will outgrow one day. I always imagined myself married to a beautiful woman, never to a man as that would be an abomination.

Going into university

My journey to self-discovery began in January 2018. I had told myself that since I will be starting university, I am going start exploring and experimenting. I promised myself that I am going to explore everything from alcohol to sex, and I did exactly that. Although I was clueless, a friend of mine introduced me to different hook-up and dating sites where I ended up meeting my virgin breaker.

On Thursday, 25 January 2018, I remember writing in my journal that it was a day I get to fully live my fantasy. I had been fantasising and hoping that one day I will get a chance to have sex with a boy. However, it was not how I imagined, but I do not really care much, I just wanted it to happen so that I can know what it felt like.

I had met a boy on the internet a few days prior and we have made an appointment. At the time, he was "straight" (heterosexual) but curious just like me. We both wanted to experiment with no strings attached. I must say that I did not know the guy, never seen him before, nor did I know his real name, but I was hosting him at my grandmother's house.

That day, I lost my virginity and my journey of self-discovery began. I slept with a "straight" stranger that I met on the internet. We both knew nothing about anal sex. He knew a thing or two about sex, I on the other hand was completely clueless. I did not know that I had to douche (clean myself). I thought it was just penetration; we both didn't know anything about lubrication so you can imagine the pain caused by friction during the penetration. It was disastrous but it was worth it. After the session that I had with the gent, I was in pain, and I was feeling guilty. I kept praying and asking for forgiveness but deep down in my heart I was happy that it happened, and I wanted more.

A few days later, I started university. I moved into my new place, staying alone. I became more curious, but I did not want to act on the curiosity because I had promised myself that I am going to start focusing on finding my wife. I believed that I went through the phase, and I am over it now. I am grown and ready to meet my future wife. Little did I know that instead of meeting my future wife, I was going to meet all the different kinds of rainbow fishes in the sea.

During my first year, apart from the sex hook-ups, I got a chance to meet amazing people. My closest friends in university contributed a lot in my journey of accepting who I am. I made two friends at that time, they were both gay and were very comfortable with their sexuality. They embraced and lived their truth. They cared less about the opinions of others. When I was around them, I felt normal. I felt happy and lighter. Every chance I got to spend with them was a chance for me to take off the "straight acting religious softie mask" and be myself. Although, behind closed doors I would hook-up with my then study partner, who taught me quite a lot about anal sex, homosexuality and sex in general.

The first 18 months of varsity I spent hooking up with different guys, exploring and experimenting with anything from weed and alcohol to sex. This was up until I met the love of my life and I have been cuffed ever since then. I have also to come out to my family because things between Brendon and I were becoming serious. He had already introduced me to his friends and family and now it was my turn. Brendon is a fictious name but represents someone I know personally.

I first came out to my brother who was very supportive. He even went to an extent of trying to ask his friend to teach me about "gay stuff" as he would say. Later, I came out to my older brother who was happy for me, but he was still reserved because he is religious, and this was "against [his] religion". A few months later, I decided to come out to my mother who throughout my childhood, was very supportive and understanding.

This is when I realised that nothing could separate us from the love of our parents except for religion. Instead of it being a joyful conversation with my mother, it became a distasteful exchange of words that turned us into enemies. Our relationship went from being good to being sour over the course of a second just because of four words – "mom, I am gay".

What I wish I knew when I was 4 was that life is going to be challenging especially because I was different, from the moment I set foot in that pre-school to now. Religion has been one of the structures that has rejected me because I don't fit the script. I see this with my mother who had been my greatest support in my formative years. My story is not unique, especially regarding religion. There has been many LGBTIQ+ teenagers who have similar experiences. What is difficult to understand now is that from 2006, when I started preferring to play with girls than boys to now where I am fully aware of my identity; nothing has changed. I see many children who are ostracised and ridiculed for being different. Instead of embracing and celebrating this uniqueness, our society rejects us. We are always in need of "intervention" to undo our identity. I wonder what the world would be like if parents and members of the community celebrated our colourful selves and created a place for us to belong? This is my story, what is yours?

Letters to our younger selves

Dear Young Katlego,

Let me start by saying, I love you very much. I can see that you are shy and scared and already at 6 years, you have seen and heard things that have traumatised you. Your life is not going to be very easy. You are going to be exposed to poverty, judgement and this will make you cry and think this is how life is supposed to be. It is not; things will be get better and one day you will start to look forward to a bright future. Know where you can draw your strength. You are everything you are going to need in this world. Don't seek validation from anyone else. Your parents love you, never doubt it.

Live your truth!

You are destined for success! Many people are going to come to you for advice not knowing that you also have so much going on in your life. You are a true beacon of hope to many and yourself. Appreciate that all that you have. It may seem gloomy along the way, but you are on the right track. Your pain is valid, and it is really time to express yourself and let people know when they have hurt you because you will realise that you carry this pain throughout. Nobody is going to come and save you.

There is so much I want to share with you, but just the thought of it, makes me emotional. I hope one day you will forgive yourself for not loving yourself.

I love you so much and I wish it were easy, but it is not. Three things I will tell you − love yourself, get that PhD and continue being the light in the lives of those around you.

XOXO

Dear Young Tshepo

I am not certain what advice you need from an older self, but I will give you some that I feel would help you appreciate and love yourself better. I've always thought of you as a smart boy, who has big dreams and a bright future ahead of him. However, I am mindful that life has its challenges, and you have to face them head on if you want to succeed. We are unfortunately born in a world where our lives and sometimes destinies are already chosen for us. You were born in a family that is a part of a community guided by what people call norms, which are to a large extent, a way of life. But there's no single way of life and this is how realities are created. In many ways, we are bound by the norms of our communities.

I want you to know one thing, there are things that you will not understand about yourself right now, but as you grow older, they will make sense and you will learn to embrace your struggles. It is okay for a boy to play with dolls, and not want anything to do with soccer. Being a boy does not mean you have to dislike what girls like. It is not about proving yourself to people but learning to accept and embrace yourself as you are. You are not a different boy, but a special kind of boy with a different identity from the other boys. Do not allow bullying to break you because it has nothing to do with you but everything to do with the bully's insecurities. They may call you names, but they don't know you. Only you know yourself and when you grow older, complete primary school and enter high school, you will realise there are certain things about yourself that will start making sense.

To my teenage self, I need you to remember that your sexuality is a special part of yourself. Don't beat yourself up or be hard on your gay self when you were still in primary and middle school; like your peers, you were also a victim of gender norms that taught you how to be a "real boy". But, like I said there's no single way of life, and just because yours is different, it doesn't make you any less of a boy. Always remember that your happiness depends on yourself, not on other people's opinions of you. So, treasure it and hold it with the highest regard, for it will be your greatest achievement in this world. Work hard on your studies, and I have no doubt that you will achieve all the success in your academics and gain all the material things that you want, but all that amounts to nothing if you are not happy. Take back your confidence from those bullies who took it away from you and show them what you are made of. It is okay to go through difficulties in life, they are what make you stronger.

To my 14-year-old self, get out of that shell that you are hiding in. You are too great to be confined to that desk and chair. It is okay to cry, but don't let them change who you are or take away the love you have for yourself. I wish I could tell you that things will get easier as you grow older, but unfortunately, they won't. You will have to become tougher and stand firm on what you believe in. The power lies within you, and every day you need to draw a bit of flame from that fire roaring inside of you to brighten up your days.

To the person I am today, I am proud of you. You've made it through life's difficulties and you continue to thrive. Life is beautiful, and you will do great things in the future. The stars are aligned, and the future is bright. Treasure your peace and share with other people the happiness that is overflowing in your heart. You are the bravest person I know and I know you have it in you to make this world a better place for many who are going through life experiences similar to yours. Forgive your past, accept apologies that you never received, and look forward to better and happier days because from here on out, your journey is filled with a whole lot of empowerment and successes. Continue searching for beautiful moments in life and most importantly believe in yourself and never stop loving yourself. Press on, even in the most difficult and unbearable of times, be kind to yourself and don't lose faith. I know you'll make it.

Love

Yours Truly

Dear Young Itumeleng

Firstly, let me start off by putting your mind at ease and let you know that you are going to be fine. Growing up, things are not always going to be great for you, but you are always going to have the right people surrounding you. You are going to grow up with a lot of insecurities, most of which you will eventually get over and embrace but who doesn't have insecurities right? My biggest advice to you is to not dim your light for the sake of others and believe in yourself because everyone around you does. You are an intelligent young man with so much to contribute so speak up and own your voice. Do not underestimate the power of your mind and your influence.

Primary school and high school are going to be some of the hardest stages of your life. You are going to feel misunderstood and isolated but never make the mistake I made and try to hide who you are for the comfort of those around you. Live fearlessly in your truth because you will later learn that this is what makes you unique and special. I urge you to fall in love with that part of your life and embrace it sooner rather than later because that is where the true beauty of who you are resides. When you get to high school you will notice something that you do not understand yourself, boys are going to make you feel in ways that you have never felt before. Know that this feeling is okay and unlike me, do not hate yourself for feeling this way despite what everyone around you says. YOU ARE PERFECT!

Mommy will send you away and although you won't understand it at first, trust me, it is for your own good. You are going to learn so much about yourself, your strengths, how to manoeuvre through life and most importantly, you will learn how to stand on your own two feet. You will realise later in life that there is a special thing about you that draws people towards you. Although this is a good thing, be careful of some people that you let into your life. Not everyone is going to have the best intentions. You will, however, meet some very good people, three of these are going to become your best friends and you will know them as soon as you meet them because their presence in your life is going to bring joy, peace, laughter, love and tons of good times. CHERISH THEM!

I would give you some advice on love and boys but that would require a whole another book altogether. I can however tell you this. You are a lover, you love love and when you love, you love hard. A lot of boys are going to come into your life and hurt you, but never allow the hurt they cause you to change how you feel about love. Allow yourself to love unapologetically and immerse yourself in the great pleasures of love. Never stop loving whole-heartedly because even if you get hurt, you will always find your way back up and love again. Love is beautiful, ENJOY IT!

Always remember, YOU ARE GOING TO BE FINE!

With Love

From the older, wiser YOU ♥

Dear Young Xola

Yours is a special journey. You are doing great. Shut out the outside noise. Shut out all that has been said to you that is negative. I want you to know that in 2021, you will have recovered and soared high. Focus your energy and attention on things that make you happy. The support you receive from your mother, father, and grandparents will help you get through all the negativity in this world. Live a precious life knowing that the Redeemer lives. You are here to stay, you are here to change the world, you are here to lead. I will always love you no matter what.

XOXO

Dear Young Obakeng,

I can already see your smile; you have just turned 14 and it pains me to see you smile like that because I know a very dark period of your life is about to start and you are going to need a lot of strength to survive it. Firstly, thank you for choosing to live, it is that decision that makes it possible to write this letter to you and that allows us to have a life that I can only describe as a trip of a lifetime. Secondly, I am not going to give you any advice, you don't need it, you don't know this yet, but you possess the gift of wisdom, you are an old soul, which makes it a little easier to navigate through life.

I am sorry but I don't have much recollection of your childhood. It is still not clear to me why this is so, but I hope to know one day. I have bits and pieces of what could possibly be memories, but I think they just stories people told me over the years. One thing I can tell you is that you were very temperamental as a child, but you were happy. Your family loved you and you loved your mom. She is the gateway to everything good you know about the world, life and yourself.

Your teenage years will be the worst years of your life. However, you will survive. There will be a series of painful events and one of them will change your life forever. Things will only start to look up when you get to 21. You will meet 3 people who will turn your world upside down in the best way possible. You will meet a boy who becomes a lifelong friend and your best friend. This friendship will become a turning point in your life. He will teach you a lot about being happy and he will protect you when you most need it; together you will make the best memories.

You will meet a white woman, whose belief in you will make you believe in the possibilities of life, and you will start doing things and taking chances. She will influence most of your career, so hold her words in your heart. They will always push you to do more in life. The third one is a surprise but believe me when I say this person will change you in ways that you never thought were humanly possible. When you meet this person, you will know it. I am sorry to tell you that this person won't stay in your life forever, but you will feel the impact they had on your life years after they have left. Make the best of this experience as it will influence most of the decisions you make in your adult years.

I know you are probably wondering about regrets and happy life; your only regret is the people whom you have hurt along the way. You will get a chance to make amends and as for a happy life, you were never unhappy, just a little lost. You have something about you that I could never really put into words; sometimes I think it is faith, sometimes I think it is resilience and sometimes I think it is God. Everything that happens is shaping you into an incredible human being. One of your blessings in life will be friends; cherish them. Your family will love and support you, show them love too. Your professional life will be interesting, be patient, it will work out. As for love, that is one thing I chose to let you find out on your own. Good luck, I am rooting for you.

P.S. You are going to be okay...

Dear Young Lerato

Hey baby boy, why are you scared? Don't be scared! There is no place for people who are scared in this world. It is a brutal world. You need to be strong. Don't let fear get in the way of you achieving your dreams. Fear will exhaust you and demotivate you from doing anything.

You are not like other boys. You are not like anyone. You have something special to offer. The world is waiting to experience what you can give. If you are afraid to speak, no one is going to hear your voice.

Remember when you want something, the universe conspires in helping you to achieve it. Dream, Run, Fight!

XOXO

Dear Young Olebogeng

I hope this letter finds you well. I am writing this letter from the future. It has been a while since we have been in touch. I just want to let you know that I have reached the future, I am living in the future. However, it is nothing like you imagined. There are no aliens or flying cars, but it seems promising.

The purpose of this letter is to tell you the things you wished you knew about the future. How things have changed, both emotionally and physically for us. I also want to give you some advice about life in general.

Like I said, things have changed drastically. Some changed for the good and some changed for the worst, but I have grown to learn that it is all part of life. Change is inevitable and is important. Apart from the "goatee" beard you have grown over the years, you are now a university graduate, you are working and most importantly you have grown to be an independent man. You are living your truth, you are embracing who you are and your sexuality. You are no longer confused, you understand things better and you understand yourself better as well. This is all good change.

Over the years you fought battles and I just want to tell you that some of those battles you fought were not yours, some were beyond you, some were not worth it, but some were essential to being who you are today.

Do not put unnecessary pressure on yourself, you are not a coal trying to become a diamond, you were born a diamond. Trying hard to fit in or belonging will only mess up your mental health. Do not act like them or try to talk like them or even try to walk like them, be you and do you! You are different and unique and those who do not appreciate you for that are not meant to be a part of your life. Over time, you will get to learn that people come and go, so do not worry yourself about friends that have become strangers.

This letter should remind you to breathe. Take one day at a time and don't be hard on yourself. Do not try to please people, focus on yourself and stay in your lane.

Remember, fortune favours the bold.

Love

Your older self

Definition of concepts

I am aware that the usage of the concepts below might mean different things to different people in different contexts. For the purposes of this book, these concepts mean the following:

Homosexuality

Homosexuality is a romantic attraction, a sexual attraction between people of the same sex or gender.

Homophobia

Homophobia refers to negative feelings, attitudes and behaviours towards individuals who are in same-sex romantic relationships, or queer bodies.

Gender

Gender is a social construct concept that refers to the roles and responsibilities of men and women in a given culture or location. These roles are influenced by perceptions and expectations arising from cultural, political, environmental, economic, social and religious factors.

Gay

Gay refers to a homosexual individual. I specifically use the term gay to refer to men attracted to other men. I am aware that the term can also be used by lesbian women.

Heterosexuality

Heterosexuality is the romantic and sexual attraction to people of opposite sex. For example, a cisgender man attracted to a cisgender woman.

Heteronormativity

This concept describes the ways in which heterosexuality is "normalised" through different practices. It assumes the gender binary.

LGBTQI

Lesbian, Gay, Bisexual, Transgender, Queer, Intersex.

Queer

Queer is an umbrella term for people who are not heterosexual.

Acknowledgements

I would like to take this opportunity to express my appreciation and gratitude towards the following individuals:

Firstly, to my loving mother and father, Tiny and Jacob Scheepers, thank you for always believing in me and for the support you have given me. Your presence in my life has taught me gratitude, love, and patience. You have shown me love even when I thought I did not deserve it. Even though at times you are not really familiar with the content of the humanities and social sciences, you have made an effort to take interest in my work.

The ever-encouraging younger sister, Tsholofelo Scheepers. Your support and encouragement touch me deeply. This serves as a testimony that it is possible. On days you think it is not working out, remember that someone before you has done it, which means you can also do it. I believe in you!

My dear confidants, Itumeleng Letlojane and Yaliwe Selebogo. All those days I was complaining, you were there for me. When I needed space, you gave it to me. You saw the importance of this book and the great impact it has for the society we live in. Thank you for allowing me to brainstorm and reading my work when I needed you to because it sometimes did not make sense.

My Lord and Saviour thank you for carrying me through the journey. On days I was frustrated, you have carried me. Prayer was my venting and you allowed me to vent. Words can never describe the love you have shown throughout this journey.

Finally, to all the contributors who took time off their busy schedule to share their stories with me. Your contribution has allowed me an opportunity to voice stories of the queer individuals in South Africa. I want to thank each and every one of you and want to say that this is the beginning of a new era for the LGBTIQ+ community across the country. I have learned so much about myself through the life accounts you shared with me. I remember with every encounter, I left energised and encouraged. You have shown me through your fighting spirit that it is all possible. One thing I will always take with me is that education is key to success. I saw myself in each and everyone of you. You have made it possible for the many that come after you. You were so open to account for every life experience.

Contributors

Katlego Scheepers is a PhD candidate at the University of Johannesburg who currently holds a master's qualification in Sociology. His research interest lies in gender, sexuality, race, and class.

Tshepo Maake is a lecturer at the University of South Africa's Department of Sociology. He completed an MA degree in Industrial Sociology (cum laude) in 2019 and is currently enrolled for a PhD degree at the University of Johannesburg. His ongoing PhD research project is entitled: Heteronormative Barriers: Constructing and Negotiating Black Gay Identities in Male-Dominated Workplaces. His research interests are masculinities, gender, sexuality, gay identities, intersectionality, heteronormativity and male-dominated workplaces.

Itumeleng Serobe is an information management specialist. He holds a BIS Information Science Degree and has just recently obtained his BA International Relations degree from the University of the Witwatersrand. His short-term goals include pursuing his postgraduate studies in International Relations and kick starting a career in International Relations and Development.

Xola Dladla-Nkosi was born and raised in Soweto. He is currently a WITS student studying Music. He expresses himself through music. He is an activist for queer lives who has made appearances on many local telenovelas in South Africa.

Obakeng Pholo is a media practitioner residing in Gauteng. He was born and raised in the North West. He is currently a news content lead for a digital media company. He has been involved in a number of initiatives that promote the inclusion of the LGBTQI+ community in corporate South Africa and is a member of the LGBTQI+ Round Table, a group of LGBTQ+ infinity groups from different corporates that aim to raise awareness about LGBTQI+ issues within corporate South Africa and also aims to contribute to an inclusive work environment.

Lerato Mofokeng was born and raised in Sebokeng, Vaal Triangle. He's currently studying towards a qualification in Law at the University of South Africa and hopes to specialise in Family Law and Law of Succession. He holds a National Diploma in Human Resources Management attained at Sedibeng TVET College. He is the owner of Capo Lerz, a clothing brand store.

Olebogeng Seripe is an enthusiastic and optimistic finance intern at one of the country's Sector Education Training Authorities. He holds a Bachelor of Financial Accountancy degree from North West University. He plans to further his studies in Financial Accounting and pursue a career as a chartered accountant.

Thatto Tshipo is a UCT theatre and performance student majoring in Scenography. A spoken word poet expressing the unspoken through voice and paper. A commercial model signed with D&A Model Management (Cape Town) and Rage Models SA (Johannesburg).